TWAYNE'S WORLD AUTHORS SERIES

A Survey of the World's Literature

Sylvia E. Bowman, Indiana University

GENERAL EDITOR

RUSSIA

Charles A. Moser, George Washington University

EDITOR

Afanasy Fet

TWAS 279

Afanasy Fet

AFANASY FET

By LYDIA M. LOTMAN

Translated from the Russian
By MARGARET WETTLIN

Prepared for publication in cooperation with
Novosti Press Agency (APN)
Publishing House, USSR

TWAYNE PUBLISHERS
A DIVISION OF G. K. HALL & CO., BOSTON

Library of Congress Cataloging in Publication Data

Lotman, Lidiia Mikhailovna.
    Afanasy Fet.

    (Twayne's world author series ; TWAS 279 : Russia)
    "Prepared for publication in cooperation with Novosti Press
Agency (APN) Publishing House, USSR."
    Bibliography: pp. 171–74
    Includes index.
    1. Shenshin, Afanasii Afanas'evich, 1820–1892.
I. Title.
PG3361.S4Z7   891.7'1'3   75–37834
ISBN 0–8057–2309–9

Contents

Translator's Note

In rendering the poems of Afanasy Fet included in this volume, the translator has tried to avoid the Scylla of a literal translation designed to provide merely the verbal sense of a given poem, and the Charybdis of a versified translation preserving the poem's exact "shape" (its pattern of rhymes and rhythm) at the expense of precise meaning.

A translation is always an altar on which, wittingly or unwittingly, something is sacrificed. A literal translation sacrifices everything but the bare bones of a poem; it is, in fact, nothing but a "trot" to ease the labors of students preparing for, say, the next French lesson.

The late Samuel Marshak called translation the transplanting of a poem from the soil of one language into that of another. It is a delicate operation, dealing as it does with such fragile materials as overtones, imagery, association, implication—wispy roots, which, if too badly damaged in the process, can cause the death of the substance, to say nothing of the spirit, of a poem. Nothing imperils these roots more seriously than the pinching and squeezing of a translation to fit the exact measurements of the original.

Yet "shape" is as integral a part of a poem as its sense; in molding the sense, it becomes inseparable from it.

Unfortunately, the prevailing custom of translating all poetry into free verse all too often results in gross misrepresentation. It is a pusillanimous habit. Surely, if the task is undertaken at all, the difficulties so plainly presented should be faced courageously.

For the purposes of this book, which does not permit too free a handling of the poetry selected to illustrate the text, the compromise has been adopted of retaining the approximate metrical structure of the poems while discarding the rhyme scheme. This approach has made possible a faithful adherence to the sequence of thoughts and images in the original (violated only when differences in language structure made it patently impossible or undesirable), without sacrificing the emotional tension inherent in the rhythm.

For the convenience of those who can read Russian, a number has been placed at the end of each poem indicating the page on which it is to be found in Fet's *Polnoe sobranie stikhotvorenii*, second edition, 1959.

MARGARET WETTLIN

Preface

Although not widely known outside his native land, Afanasy Fet enjoys a considerable reputation within it as one of the finest Russian lyric poets of the nineteenth century.

Fet's reputation has fluctuated over the decades which have passed since his first collection of verse was published in the early 1840's. His talent was early recognized by such men as Vissarion Belinsky, Russia's greatest nineteenth-century critic, who wrote: "Of all the Moscow poets, Fet is the most gifted."[1] And another of Russia's finest critical minds, Apollon Grigorev, himself a poet and personal friend of Fet's, said of his work that "there is much of us, much of the perturbation of our own hearts in this poetry."[2] Such acclaim, however, did not prove constant: in the 1860's Belinsky's critical followers banished Fet from the ranks of true poets, mocking him as the perfect example of what a writer should not be and do at a time when social problems were deemed of overriding importance. Fet then suffered an eclipse which lasted several decades: not until the turn of the century did he begin to come into his own once more. Then he became a principal influence upon the course of Russian poetry, and his place has remained firm and steady through most of the Soviet period.

In this study Lydia Lotman deals in detail with the history of Fet's poetic development. She analyzes his first collection, in which he showed by his relatively imitative style that he had not yet discerned his true literary path. She emphasizes the Russian quality of his poetic vision and reminds us that he spent much of his life far from the country's cosmopolitan literary capital, St. Petersburg. She investigates his faith in nature and its reflection in his poetry. She discusses the explicit formulation of his esthetics in critical articles which he felt compelled to write in the late 1850's and early 1860's under the challenge of radical literary doctrine. She also takes up the implicit philosophy of his art as expressed in his poems:

his thoughts on the possibility of verbal communication through poetry even while he insisted on divorcing poetry from philosophy as a matter of principle; his poems on poetry; his poems on music. And when she comes to the last decade or so of Fet's life, she analyzes for us the ruminations on life, death, and the meaning of existence which became so prominent in his work then.

Fet was deeply interested in philosophy, especially that of Schopenhauer, whom he translated into Russian. He was not by any means what is ordinarily termed a "philosophical" poet. Yet philosophy and poetry were intertwined at a less explicit level in his work, and that connection is one which Lydia Lotman elucidates in this study.

The "Conclusion" summarizes Fet's influence upon his poetic descendants and his role in the history of Russian poetry after his death.

This book is not the first on Fet to appear in English, but it has much to offer both by way of utilizing previous scholarship on Fet and by way of original interpretation. It makes a valuable contribution to our understanding of the course of nineteenth-century Russian literature.

• • •

The author, Lydia Lotman, is a Soviet research scholar in philology at the Leningrad Institute of Russian Literature, a branch of the USSR Academy of Sciences. She is the author of a book on the leading nineteenth-century Russian playwright Alexander Ostrovsky. Among her other publications are contributions to multi-volume Soviet histories of Russian literature, of Russian criticism, of the Russian novel, and of Russian poetry. These contributions include the articles "Novels of Folk Life and Ethnographical Novels," "Pisemsky as Novelist," "The Democratic Tendency in Russian Poetry of the 1850's, 1860's, and 1870's," and "Lyrical and Historical Poetry of the 1850's, 1860's, and 1870's." She compiled the collection of Ostrovsky's verse dramas for the "Poet's Library" edition and helped to edit and supply commentary for collections of works by Nikolay Gogol, Mikhail Lermontov, Vissarion Belinsky, and Ivan Turgenev.

—The Editor

Chronology

1820 Afanasy Shenshin brings Charlotta Elizaveta Foeth (Fet) from Darmstadt, Germany, where she had lived with her husband I. P. Foeth, to "Novosyolki," his estate in Russia near the town of Mtsensk. November 28: The future poet Afanasy Fet is born at "Novosyolki." His father illegally registers him as his son.

1822 Shenshin marries Charlotta Fet.

1835 After discovering that Fet was born before Elizaveta Fet and Afanasy Shenshin were legally married, the ecclesiastical authorities annul the birth documents. On the basis of an affidavit sent from Darmstadt, the Orlov Consistory issues a document stating that Afanasy was "the son of tax-assessor I. P. Foeth and his former wife Charlotta Foeth."

1835– Fet attends the Krümmer boarding school in the town
1837 of Verro (now Vyru), Estonia.

1838 Fet enters the Law faculty of Moscow University; later transfers to the Philological Section of the Philosophical Department of the same University.

1840 Fet's first book of verse, the *Lyrical Pantheon*, is published over the signature A. F.

1841– Fet publishes poems in the journals *The Muscovite* and
1842 *Notes of the Fatherland*.

1844 Fet graduates from the University. July–August goes to Darmstadt and Frankfurt-on-Main. Begins writing for the journal *Repertoire and Pantheon*.

1845 Joins a regiment of cuirassiers stationed in Novogeorgievsk in the Ukraine. Nikolay I issues a manifesto stating that the right to become a member of the hereditary nobility can be earned only upon reaching a senior officer's rank, which means Fet would have to wait fifteen or twenty years instead of the six months he had counted on.

1847   During a vacation in Moscow, Fet prepares a collection of verse for the press. December: The collection is passed by the censor.

1848   In late summer and early autumn, becomes friendly with Mariya Lazich.

1850   At the beginning of the year, Fet's new collection appears. Summer: Death of Mariya Lazich (a suspected suicide).

1852   Beginning of Fet's connection with *The Contemporary*.

1853   Transferred to a Guard Regiment of Uhlans stationed in Krasnoe Selo, near St. Petersburg.

1854   Makes the acquaintance of, and is accepted into, the literary circle of *The Contemporary*. Friendship with Turgenev. A period of great creative activity. February 22: Fet's regiment sent to Estonia to guard the Baltic coast.

1856   A new collection of Fet's verse, edited by Turgenev, is passed by the censor. From June to December, a European trip to Germany, France, Italy. A new *ukase* issued, delaying still further the bestowal of hereditary nobility through service as an army officer. For Fet, the award is now unattainable. June: Fet resigns from the army, travels abroad. August 16: marries Mariya Petrovna Botkina, sister of the literary critic Vasily Botkin.

1860–   Purchases "Stepanovka," an estate in the Mtsensk dis-
1861   trict; devotes himself to reconstructing the house and supervising the land.

1862   Two articles entitled "Notes on Free Labor" published in *The Russian Herald*.

1863   A new collection of Fet's works appears.

1863–   Three articles entitled "Notes from the Village" pub-
1864   lished in *The Russian Herald*. Radical critics attack Fet's articles, review his 1863 collection unfavorably.

1873   December 23: Alexander II grants Fet permission to take the name of Shenshin.

1882   The collection *Evening Lights* passed by the censor.

1883   Fet's translations of Horace published.

1884   A second edition of *Evening Lights* passed by the censor.

Chronology

1885   Fet's translation of Schopenhauer's treatise *The Four-fold Root of the Principle of Sufficient Reason* published.

1886   Fet's translations of Catullus appear.

1887   Third edition of *Evening Lights* passed by the censor.

1888   Publication of Fet's translation of Schopenhauer's *World as Will and Idea*, Propertius' *Elegies*, Part II of Goethe's *Faust*, and Part II of Vergil's *Aeneid*.

1889   Fet awarded title of Chamberlain.

1890   Volumes I and II of Fet's *Memoirs* published. Fourth edition of *Evening Lights* passed by the censor.

1892   Work on memoirs *The Early Years*, published posthumously in 1893. November 21: Death of the poet. November 25: Buried on the Shenshin estate in the province of Orlov.

CHAPTER 1

The Poet Embarks

I Lyrical Pantheon

IN 1840, Afanasy Fet made his literary debut by publishing at his own expense a volume of verse pretentiously entitled *Liricheskii panteon* (*Lyrical Pantheon*) and modestly signed "A. F." Life had not been kind to this twenty-year-old student. At the age of fourteen he had discovered he was not the eldest son of the proud and influential Russian landowner Afanasy Shenshin, as he had hitherto believed, but the son of an obscure German tax assessor, named Foeth (Fet).

The popularity of the young poet's verse among his fellow students and the appreciation of it expressed by Nikolay Gogol,[1] who during the 1830's and 1840's was the idol of Russian youth, inspired Fet with romantic hopes of making his way in the world with the money received from the sale of his poems.

These hopes were soon dashed. He would never forget the humiliating experience of soliciting funds for the publication of this first volume of his, and the reproaches of his stern step-father, Afanasy Shenshin, who gave him to understand that his plans and aspirations were childishly naïve. This coincided with his first disappointment in love, rejection by a poor governess to whom he had given his heart!

To these early disappointments Fet dedicated his poem "Kol'tso" ("The Ring"), which conveys his fleeting exhilaration, followed by a persistent distrust of the future. The agonizing presentiment that happiness would never be his, his acceptance of the stoic ideal, his early conception of universal harmony—all these foreshadow the mature poet.

> My heart makes answer in your stead,
> And now I kiss you, friendly ring,

Symbol of eternal life; this endless circle
Pledges to me a golden immortality. . . .

Happiness, away! I know you not.
We two are bound by nothing but this ring.
Here, sea—accept my gift,
For which you long have clamored.
So sharp a change from calm to storm
Shall find no least reflection on my face.
Now light my heart. Gone is my ring,
Gone too the last poor spark of hope
Within this breast.[2]

"The Ring" is one of the poems included in the *Lyrical Pantheon*. A beginner's diffidence is revealed in the traditional forms Fet uses and in the imitativeness of many of the pieces, whose themes, imagery, phrases, and rhythms remind us now of Alexander Pushkin, now of Vasily Zhukovsky, Mikhail Lermontov or Vladimir Benediktov. It is as if the poet had set himself the task of trying his hand at all the popular forms of the day: Romantic medieval ballads in the spirit of Zhukovsky ("Raufenbach Castle"); oriental ballads in imitation of Lermontov ("Abducted from the Harem"); drinking songs; and love lyrics.

Yet even in this first collection there are intimations of the new and distinguished style that was to be Fet's own. If at times he imitates Benediktov, it is always with reserve, avoiding in his own work the vulgar excesses of the older poet. Fet's rejection of the pomposity that many authors of romances confused with elevated feeling, his powers of close observation, and the use of only his own personal feelings and experiences in his writing established a deep affinity between him and the young writers of the 1840's, who were intent on discovering new means of depicting the men and the world of their own day.

Fet treated the purely Romantic subject of his ghost ballad "Udavlennik" ("The Hanged Man") as an episode from real life, a tale told by a simple and superstitious man. One perceives Pushkin's influence here—his ballad "Utoplennik" ("The Drowned Man") and "Funeral Song" from *Songs of the Western Slavs*. The credulous storyteller of "The Hanged Man" and the horrors he relates, obviously reflecting the gullibility of the simple folk, are set in surroundings recalling the poet's own:

> Supper is over. Thank the Lord
> All are ready and gathered at last.
> Come, sit silent here a moment
> For Godspeed. Then off we go! (373)

The family is seeing their son off on a long journey (as if it were Fet himself leaving for boarding school). As they choose the road he is to take, they tell him about the ghost of a man who hanged himself and rises from his grave to frighten travelers. It is not difficult to surmise that Fet took many of the hair-raising details of this story from the accounts given by the house servants at Novosyolki (the Shenshin estate where he spent his childhood) of how a neighboring landowner had been hanged by his serfs. In his memoirs, Fet says: "The story of the murder of this neighbor, with whom we were well acquainted, grew into an epic poem to which each new narrator added details and coloring. I am unable to identify the contributions of the innumerable people who created the poem. I can only give it in the form in which it reached my youthful ears."[3]

"The Hanged Man" was not merely an imitative work. Its atmosphere was taken less from Fet's reading of Zhukovsky and the German poets than from his own observations. Among his fellow-students at school were the sons of a wealthy Baltic baron named Pereir. These boys once took Fet home with them during vacation and visited the boys' grandfather, whose luxurious mansion and grounds, the latter including a graveyard with ancient tombs and vaults, made an indelible impression on Fet. In his memoirs he gives a detailed description of the buildings on the estate and of his adventures in one of the vaults.[4]

The sense of reality and genuine feeling behind Fet's descriptions and lyrics, his presentation of native scenes without exaggerated coloring, and the emotional reserve maintained throughout the book, distinguish the poems of the *Lyrical Pantheon* from the imitative, Romantic productions of other apprentice poets of that day. Fet himself was aware that simplicity was the basic attribute of his poetry. He compared his muse to an unaffected maiden in simple attire: "An air of simplicity en-

velops my muse." Simplicity was fundamental to Fet's conception of the beautiful, testifying to his sincerity and daring, and
to his acceptance of Pushkin as his poetic ideal. His poem
"Uzh, serpy na plecha vzlozhiv, ustalye zhnetsy . . ." ("At Even-
tide the Weary Reapers . . ."; with an epigraph from Horace:
"Nec sit ancillae tibi amor pudori," "Be not ashamed of thy
love for a slave") presents, in the slow measure of Russian
hexameter (dactyls combined with trochees), a picture of
evening in a Russian village. It concludes by describing the
sufferings of a youth who falls in love with a peasant girl he
glimpses beside a stream. The poet's precise, unambiguous use
of adjectives renders physical objects concrete and visible, brings
them, as it were, into sharp focus: "weary reapers," "cool field,"
"scrubby bushes," "old and spreading willow." He creates
homely images to convey the living spirit of evening in his
native village.

> The wood is fragrant with lilies; above the ravine the birches
> Are rosy with sunset light; here in these scrubby bushes
> A nightingale sings, welcoming the coolness of evening. (398)

In Alexander Blok's copy of Fet's verse, the lines from this
poem "My trusty mount steps slowly ahead . . . Brushing away
the gnats with his tail" are underscored. Blok seems to have
found them trite. He underscored another unhappy line in the
poem "K leshemu" ("To the Wood Goblin"), although on the
whole this poem pleased him, as well it might, having much
in common with Blok's own "Bolotnym popikam" ("Little Priests
of the Bog"). In this poem, Fet presents the woodland sprites
and goblins of Russian folklore, which the modern sculptor
Sergey Konenkov discovered and to which he gave permanent
form in the gnarled roots of trees. Despite the classical conven-
tionality of the love theme in this miniature poem, "To the
Wood Goblin" conveys a genuine impression of the woods and
the poet's response to nature.

Many of the pieces in the *Lyrical Pantheon* are introduced by
epigraphs indicating that the young poet was presenting his
own conception of an idea already treated by an older poet.
His "Solntse potukhlo, plavaet zapakh . . ." ("The Sun Is Low,

Sweet Scents Are Wafting...") develops the theme of Pushkin's "Vesna, vesna, pora liubvi" ("The Spring, the Spring, the Time of Love!"), which serves as epigraph. Fet's "Ty mne prostish, moi drug, chto kazhdyi chas..." ("Forgive Me, My Friend, If Every Time...") is a story in verse illustrating Horace's "Amantium irae amoris renovatio..." ("Lovers' quarrels feed the flames of love..."). The characters in the story are the poet, his young friend, and his friend's beloved. The author casts the light of irony upon the feelings and relationships of those involved in this little incident. The sweethearts quarrel, but their quarrel is feigned as a means of veiling and justifying a wild upsurge of love. Behind the indignant lover's demand that the poet sympathize with him in his suffering is his desire that the poet be witness to his happiness. The poet, enchanted by this evidence of true feeling, is ironic about the Romantic pretense of estrangement, the mask of disappointment the lovers vainly attempt to wear:

> I say, what a droll picture you make at the window,
> In slippers and dressing gown, smoking a cigar cheroot:
> Aleko, Mortimer, ah yes, Othello,
> And even a hint of Hamlet! (395)

There is amusement in Fet's identification of his friend with all these literary heroes: the complaining lover was probably more like the ordinary young men of Fet's acquaintance. Horace's aphorism, then, becomes the point of departure for a story about Fet's contemporaries, their whims and fancies, the manners and feelings characteristic of their day, and the relationship of young people to one another. Fet felt that he himself had "a hint of Hamlet" in him, but with respect to himself this feeling was not only without irony but often deeply tragic, as expressed in his later poems.

Richard F. Gustafson, the American critic, has correctly noted that in the poem "Vodopad" ("The Waterfall"), which was included in the *Lyrical Pantheon,* Fet expresses his opposition to the Romantic point of view. In this poem, Fet handles a favorite theme in Russian poetry. Gustafson compares Fet's poem with poems on the same subject by Gavriil Derzhavin and Evgeny

Baratynsky and concludes that Fet's treatment is distinguished
by the peculiar reality of his imagery. He perceives objects
spatially. He juxtaposes two conflicting concepts: the dark and
chaotic depths at the foot of the waterfall, and the placid
waters of the river flowing in the distance, intimating that this
calm distance is the harmony toward which man aspires.[5]

In "The Waterfall," the young poet demonstrates his careful
study of Pushkin's artistic achievements. In its composition and
structural characteristics the poem is akin to Pushkin's "Kavkaz"
("The Caucasus"). Pushkin, and subsequently Fet, survey the
majestic scenery from above. Pushkin sees in it "the source of
life," watches, as through storm clouds, the "thunderous fall
of the stream," and then, allowing his eye to travel the length
and breadth of the valley, focuses it upon the river flowing
between cliffs. This is not a placid river, contrasting, like Fet's,
with the chaos of the waterfall, but rather a mountain stream
caught between walls of rock and wildly protesting against its
confinement. It is not the idea but the structure of the poem
that enables us to see in it the prototype of Fet's "Waterfall."

It is of great significance that behind Pushkin's powerful
description of the grandeurs of waterfall and mountains lay a
philosophical concept that gave metaphorical significance to the
scenery. In his first version, Pushkin revealed such a philosophical plane by the use of direct comparison rather than metaphor. That version ended in the following lines:

> Thus does the law curb the wild and the free,
> Thus do they languish 'neath foreign oppression.
> Thus the mute Caucasus nurses resentment,
> Thus is it blighted by alien rule.[6]

There is good reason to apply a philosophical interpretation
to Fet's "Waterfall" as well. As the poet contemplated the rebellious waters confined within overhanging cliffs and blocked by
a granite boulder as by "a felled Titan," then raised his eyes to
where the stream flowed quietly between low banks in the distance, he was reminded of the circumstances of his own life
and his hopes for the future; to him, the movement of the
stream represented the movement of human life in time. Perhaps

the free-flowing river expressed his youthful faith in life's wisdom and beneficence, and that is why the mood of the poem is
bright and uplifting.

In the *Lyrical Pantheon,* the young poet introduced themes
and images to which he reverted repeatedly in his later work.
By the time Fet's poetry had freed itself of literary clichés and
acquired its characteristic precision of description and depth
of psychological motivation, these recurrent themes and images
had been enriched by elaborate associations and philosophical
connotations.

We have already spoken of Fet's predilection for the circle
image, which first appeared in his poem "The Ring." In his
translation of Goethe's "May Song" he introduces it again, even
though Goethe does not make direct use of it in the original.
"Is it not thou, Love, who hast attired Nature in fine raiment,
who hast blessed the meadows and cast thy radiance upon this
earthly sphere?" "Sphere" in this case refers to space encircling
all of mankind rather than the application of "ring" or "circle"
to a given individual. In Fet's later poems, this favorite image
is used predominantly to indicate the individual's environment,
the "circle" in which he lives and moves, and which has its own
peculiar moral atmosphere.

The poem "Moi sad" ("My Garden") represents another first
appearance of images that appear again and again in Fet's later
poetry. Gustafson is inclined to accept this poem as a symbolic
expression of the philosophical essence of Fet's poetry.[7] To this
critic, the images of the garden and eternal spring represent
Fet's rejection of real life with its prosaic concerns and its
struggles.

It is true that "My Garden" anticipates a frequent use of
this theme in Fet's succeeding work and suggests the philosophical view that man's perception of beauty in nature, in
human relations, and in art is something apart from the rest
of human life. On the other hand, the very understanding of
beauty as expressed in this poem is so like that of all Romantic
poets, and Fet's world of imagery is so directly connected with
all that had been produced before him, that "My Garden"
is more nearly the garden of Romantic poetry in general (very
like the garden in Heine's *Buch der Lieder,* of which Fet was

so fond) than a revelation of a secret world belonging to Fet
alone.

As we shall see later, nature became for Fet a means of ap-
prehending and defining the beautiful instead of merely a
stimulus leading the poet to give expression to a fixed order of
esthetic images corresponding to an accepted artistic platform.

"Vzdokh" ("The Sigh") gives the first indication of a trend
that can be traced in all of Fet's succeeding poetry. The name
itself is unusual, yet typical of Fet. It reveals something unique
in his conception. He does not write about a person who sighs;
the poem is itself a sigh, a spontaneous and involuntary lyrical
impulse. Brief, expressed as it were in one breath, it instantly
captures an idea emerging from a prolonged state of melancholy.

This use of a single, trenchant word as title to supplement,
even elucidate a poem, was often employed by Fet later—as for
example, "Dal'" ("Distance"), "Nikogda" ("Never"), "Teper'"
("Now").

If, then, in the *Lyrical Pantheon* the young poet is clearly a
beginner taking his cue from older masters, there are also definite
signs of his creative individuality. This individuality is expressed, among other ways, in the choice of teachers he wished
to follow, in his selection of the Pushkin tradition as his guide,
and in his interest in world poetry, especially Latin verse
(Horace in particular) and German verse, with which even at
this early date he was thoroughly familiar.

II *The Period Following the* Lyrical Pantheon

Fet did not expect that the appearance of his modest first
collection would create a sensation, but he did hope it would
be noticed by the critics, and he took steps to ensure this out-
come. His energetic nature led him to such action, as did his
realization that a good review of his work was essential to the
continuation of his literary activities, which alone, he felt, could
extricate him from his material difficulties and offer him a distinguished career. He was further impelled by his fear of the
relentless critic Belinsky, writing in the journal *Notes of the
Fatherland,* who had directed his devastating pen even against
Benediktov, the idol of the day. He appealed to his friend,

Irinarkh Vvedensky, then on the staff of the popular magazine *Library for Reading,* who had promised to help him. Fet confided to him his reasons for wanting a good review of the *Lyrical Pantheon*: "I must confess that I greatly fear *Notes of the Fatherland* and the ogre Belinsky.... God willing, I shall devote myself exclusively to literary activities; if this proves impossible I will be in a bad way indeed. My soul is poisoned by circumstances revoltingly sordid."[8]

Irinarkh Vvedensky promised Fet the review, but instead of Vvedensky it was eventually written by Osip Senkovsky, a well-known journalist on the editorial board of the *Library for Reading*. The review was annihilating. This disappointment, however, was compensated for by the unexpectedly favorable reaction from *Notes of the Fatherland*. Though written by Pyotr Kudryavtsev, the review was inspired by Belinsky. Both these estimates of the *Lyrical Pantheon* and its author, though written from opposite viewpoints, were sufficiently astute to detect qualities that became typical of Fet's later work. Senkovsky observed sarcastically that at the center of all the poems stood the poet's ego. "A pantheon," he wrote, "is a temple of the gods—that I know, but I must confess my ignorance of what a lyrical pantheon is. A temple to lyrical gods?" he asked, by way of scoffing at the volume's pretentious title. In his opinion, the author reserved all the niches in the pantheon for himself.[9] He asserted that the poetic images in the book lacked harmony and divine inspiration. "This is no pantheon!" he exclaimed. "More like pandemonium! A temple to imps and devils!" He was particularly incensed by the poem "To the Wood Goblin." After citing it, he expressed his incredulity that the poet could associate this malicious sprite of folk demonology with love. Later we shall see that this association, which Senkovsky felt was a chance one, became the central image of a whole cycle of Fet's poems.

Another observation in Senkovsky's short and unfavorable review deserves attention. He accused Fet of despising logical thinking. Fet was subjected to this same accusation at various times thereafter, and in the excitement of rebuttal the poet often spoke testily of "the logic of prosaic practical thinking" as opposed to "the bard's wild flights of fancy."

Kudryavtsev's opinion was shared by the editorial board of
Notes of the Fatherland: in one of his letters, Belinsky supports
Kudryavtsev's appraisal of the young "A. F.'"s talent. Kudryavtsev found the greatest virtues of the poems to be the simplicity
and modesty of their language (the very attributes with which
Fet had endowed his muse), their loyalty to the traditions
of the best masters, and their freedom from Romantic exaggera-
tion. He selected the anthological poems as the most significant
and promising but also praised the translations from Goethe
and Horace, noting at the same time that the author showed
inadequate knowledge of the Greek poets, despite an intuitive
feeling for the ancient world, demonstrated in his poem "Greece."
This last criticism went straight to the mark: as a student at
Moscow University, Fet had been required to spend two years
in the third course owing to his failure in classical Greek.

After quoting from Fet's anthological lyrics, Kudryavtsev
exclaimed: "What is the source of such marvelous imagery? . . .
But indeed it matters little whether it comes from inborn talent
nurtured on the deathless poetry of the past, or simply from
inherent delicacy, an inherent feeling for nature; the main thing
is that it lives! We cordially welcome the appearance of this
new poet."[10]

Belinsky, from whom Fet had feared the worst, felt that the
reviewer's occasional references to the poet's youth and in-
experience were uncalled for. "What a fine review he gave of
Fet's *Lyrical Pantheon!*" wrote Belinsky. "Only he was too spar-
ing of his praise. Oh, stern critic! A. F. shows great promise."[11]

Soon Fet himself became highly critical of his first book.
One of the few writers of his day capable of accepting criticism,
he learned a lesson not only from Kudryavtsev's sympathetic
remarks, but also from Senkovsky's taunts. To be sure, then as
later, the only advice Fet accepted was that which helped him
elucidate and perfect his own artistic method and which was
pointed in the direction of his own creative strivings. He immediately admitted the pretentiousness of the title of his first
book, and his next three collections appeared in print merely
as *Poems by A. A. Fet.* He included only four of the poems
from the *Lyrical Pantheon* in his second book and only two—
both lyrics in the classical style—in succeeding collections.

The poem "Greece," which had won praise from Kudryavtsev, was included in every succeeding collection and was supplemented, in the second one, by a series of translations from the Greek, which Fet, taking his critic's advice, had learned more thoroughly.

Fet's complete absorption in the writing of poetry made him long to have his poems reach the public. This was no easy undertaking. Over a period of several years, his efforts to publish in periodicals were vain. The frustrated poet's greatest consolation lay in his friendship with Apollon Grigorev, a poet who would become a leading critic. On calmly receiving the news of Grigorev's death many years later, when the two had long since parted company and their lives had followed different paths, Fet recalled the years of their youth and their poetic rapport:

Never have I had such a jealous admirer and collector of my first drafts as Apollon. Soon after I went to live in his house my old yellow notebook was replaced by a new one in which my poems were meticulously written in Apollon's hand.

At times my inspiration was born of the dreariness of our empty lives that oppressed both of us.

Once he exclaimed, "God! Just take a look at that stove, that table with the burnt-out candle on it, those frozen windows! It's enough to drive a person mad!"

It was then I wrote the little poem, "Do not fret, my pretty kitty ..." which Apollon took a great fancy to. He had an ear as sensitive as an Aeolian harp. I remember the raptures he went into over the little piece, "My kitten is singing, eyes shut tight. . . ." "How happy the cat and how miserable the child!" he exclaimed.[12]

Not merely individual poems (though there were many of them), but whole cycles were inspired by moods shared with Apollon Grigorev at the beginning of the 1840's. Fet himself has told us that the classification of his poems into cycles was Grigorev's work. In this way the cycles "Melancholy" and "To Ophelia" seem to have evolved. "Occasionally one meets with ties like ours—for better or for worse," wrote Grigorev in later years. "For a moment of merging with that proud, that feminine, that masculinely-noble soul, for the rare evenings when we were perfectly attuned to each other, I thank Providence more—oh, a thousand times more!—than for my whole life."[13]

Naturally, many of the cycles composed at the beginning of the 1840's were an expression of Fet's own creative aspirations, independent of his friend's mood. This is true of the somber cycle "Snega" ("Snow"), describing country scenes and life in a remote village, and partly true of "Gadaniia" ("Fortune-telling").

At one time both friends were enamored of Heinrich Heine's poetry. In an article written in 1853, Grigorev speaks of the spiritual affinity between the lyrical themes treated by Heine and by Fet. As a talented critic who knew and loved Fet personally, Grigorev perceived that both Fet and Heine suffered from a gnawing egoism, that their inner world was tragically shattered, and that their restraint and withdrawal, their attempt to hide or disguise their feelings, was the result of a painful modesty.[14]

Without mentioning the kinship between his own and Heine's muses, Fet, with characteristic reticence, speaks in a purely professional way of certain similarities of Heine's style to his own: "nobody . . . ever exercised such power over me as Heine, and this was because of his manner of speaking not of the influence of one object upon another, but only of the objects themselves, forcing the reader to sense their relationship; for example, the weeping daughter of the dead forester and the dog curled at her feet."[15] Here, Fet declares the importance he attached to the "objectification" of intimate, subjective emotions, the search for those forms taken from the real world which, given artistic representation, evoke in the reader the poet's feelings and impressions. In memoirs written toward the end of his life he notes the importance of his youthful artistic searchings, which led him to an important discovery in the field of verse form. It was in this early period that Fet began working on miniatures in which the poet conveyed emotion by presenting an objective picture of the world about him.

Heine's experience as a poet was of particular interest to Fet during the period when he was developing his professional skill and seeking new devices of poetic expression. In the short poems he wrote at the beginning of the 1840's, he fixes a certain moment in the constant flux and flow of impressions, a moment lending impetus to the development of feeling and the birth of ideas. But even then the poet pondered the problem of the "content" of time and tried to "expand" time by compressing impressions, emotions, and sensations within a given moment.

Boris Bukhshtab, a Soviet scholar, discovered in the Betskov archives of the Lenin Library in Moscow a list of poems compiled by Fet; the poems belonged to a cycle called "Mgnoveniia" ("The Fleeting Moment"), which Fet gave to Stepan Shevyrov in 1842 for publication in the magazine *Moskvitianin* (*The Muscovite*). Only two of the poems on the list appeared in that magazine, the rest being published only in 1859. The cycle is interesting primarily because its theme is "time," the basic unit of which is "the fleeting moment." The cycle includes the poems "Khronos" ("Chronos") and "Strannaia uverennost" ("Strange Conviction"), which in idea, imagery, and poetical structure resemble Pushkin's "Telega zhizni" ("The Wagon of Life") and "Zoriu b'iut," ("Day Is Rung In . . ."), as well as the elegy "Zhelanie" ("Desire"); and poems which in form correspond to the title, "The Fleeting Moment," and are analogous, in another genre, to Sergey Prokofiev's musical compositions of the same name ("The Fleeting Moment").

All the poems in this cycle treat of time in its tragic aspect, expressed in traditional, symbolic images: life is an open road, time is the coachman, each separate day is a segment of the road that leads to eternity. Fet's conclusion as to this traditional treatment is somewhat unexpected: the meaning of life consists in leaving some memory of oneself behind. This is the end to be reached in life's long and exhausting journey, but even this end, this snatching of "a fleeting moment" from eternity (the individual persists if but in a fleeting memory) is ephemeral, as is intimated by the name of the poem, "Strange Conviction." Fet's philosophical poem, "Chronos", seems to be intentionally senseless. The very essence of life is senselessness, the never-ending exchange of one instant for the next. The poem concludes with the line: "When the twelfth hour strikes, the first begins."

Each poem in the cycle "The Fleeting Moment" is devoted

to some passing impression: the expectation of reunion in parting
in "Vozvrashchenie" ("Return"); a vision of the beloved in the
window in "Eyo okno" ("Her Window"); a prayer ("Ave
Maria"). The fleeting quality of emotions is most vividly expressed in the two poems "Perchatka" ("The Glove") and
"Sorvalsia moi kon'" ("My Steed Has Fled"). "The Glove" is
a delicate miniature narrating the hero's infatuation at a ball,
his following from afar the "sweet-smelling circle of her influence" into which he suddenly finds himself drawn. The only
memory that remains of this fleeting passion is the glove he keeps.

The two quatrains comprising "My Steed Has Fled" violate
Fet's principle that "a short poem should have but a single
core."[16] In the poem in question the violation is fully justified.
The first quatrain describes the excitement and alarm attending
a youth's discovery that his horse has fled from the stable. He
rushes in pursuit, shouting for help, but suddenly he spies a
neighbor's daughter, who has come to the window in response
to his cries (her name and his manner of address suggest that
she is a simple country girl). Forgetting all about the horse,
he calls wonderingly to those who have come to his aid: "Look,
oh look! / Pasha has come to the window!"

The instantaneous change of the youth's emotions transforms
those who have come to assist him into confidants to whom he
reveals the state of his heart. Such a shifting of theme harmo-
nizes with the idea of the cycle, which is to capture fleeting
moments, showing their endless succession and their shifting
of content. The precision and compactness of the story, focusing
upon a simple exclamation of surprise, the spontaneous emotional response to an unexpected situation, is only another
means of conveying the "fleetingness" of events and the hero's
instantaneous response to them. The form of the verse in this
cycle corresponds to its content, since most of the poems consist
of only two or three quatrains, using two- or three-foot lines of
iambs or anapests. The poem to which Fet first gave the name
"Desire" ("Dear God, how much of this my life I'd sacrifice. . .")
is an exception. A note written in Fet's hand in the margin of
the list of poems belonging to the cycle indicates his doubt
that this particular poem should be included. "I was mistaken
when I included this song, this elegy, among the others," he

wrote. The poem is indeed a typical Fet "love song," written
in flowing rhythm (iambic hexameter). But even in this poem
the lyrical theme is interwoven with the time theme, the "long"
moment juxtaposed with the "brief" eternity.

> Dear God, how much of this my life I'd sacrifice
> To spend alone with her one quiet Northern evening,
> To silently commune in language of the eyes,
> To call her mine if but for one brief Northern evening.

A whole life may be contained in a single evening, and endless
days may not be as valuable as one short experience; and this
because in a few precious hours there may occur the miracle
of realizing one's individuality in all its richness, the miracle
of a complete spiritual renascence, the miracle of meeting
and recognizing another and a kindred soul.

> To see a tear form slowly in her eye,
> The tear I have reflected on so often,
> And to respond to everything with all my soul—
> To everything so richly given her by Heaven.

The concept of a "precious hour" representing a segment
of time whose qualitative uniqueness effects a quantitative
change (the "long" moment, hour, evening) thereafter became
a dominant idea in Fet's lyrics.

CHAPTER 2

Literary Recognition

I *The Collection of 1850 and Its Structure*

IN November of 1841 three translations from Heine and two original poems, signed "A. F.," were published in *The Muscovite*. Later Fet became a permanent contributor to the journal. His poems immediately attracted attention. Fet was invited to contribute to other journals, and by the middle of 1842 was being published by the radical *Notes of the Fatherland*, as well as by the conservative *Muscovite*. The literary coterie of that period attracted him primarily as the sphere of professional writers. He made the acquaintance of men of letters representing various political views and trends, and enjoyed the opportunity of calling on such different figures as Professor Shevyrov of the conservative Slavophiles, and Avdotya Glinka, a woman whose name became symbolic of antagonism toward all that was contemporary in literature, especially as represented by Belinsky's radical group. Fet attended the salon of Mikhail Pavlov, where he met such men as Timofey Granovsky and Alexander Herzen, dedicated to the westernization of Russian culture. He embraced literature as a fascinating field of activity, whose main interest for him lay in the professional problems it presented.

At the same time he was not beyond taking political sides. Indeed, he was so incensed by a reactionary poem written by a certain Dmitriev against Belinsky that, in collaboration with Grigorev—in Bukhshtab's opinion—he wrote a scathing poem in reply. Belinsky was highly pleased with this demonstration of the students' sympathy with his ideas.[1] In Fet's poem the diehard older generation, which, convinced of the sacredness of class and serfdom, rejected the humanitarian tendencies of contemporary art as embodied in the poetry of Pushkin, is confronted with the "common sense" of the younger generation. The portrait of these reactionary fathers presented in the poem shows a striking resemblance to Fet's stepfather, Afanasy Shenshin, as he was later described in Fet's memoirs.

When Fet graduated from Moscow University in 1844, he was faced with the necessity of choosing an occupation. In that same year he journeyed to Darmstadt, Germany, to make the acquaintance of his German relatives and bring his sister to Russia. During this trip an incident of no small importance occurred. Once while he was taking a boat trip from Stettin to Swinemünde, the orchestra, as a favor to the Russian passengers, played Alexander Varlamov's song "Awake Her Not at Break of Day."[2] This song was a setting to music of Fet's poem, although everyone in Russia as well as in Germany took it for a Russian folk song. This curious fact was noted by Apollon Grigorev in 1850.[3] Fet's contemporaries sought and found his poems on the pages of magazines, and yet the poet felt that he was poor, unknown, and facing a frightening future. His family had decided he was to enter the army, since at that time this career offered the quickest means of becoming a member of the nobility. But during his visit to Darmstadt he was informed of the death of his stepfather's brother, Pyotr Shenshin, who had promised to use his influence in securing him a regimental post. By his death Fet was deprived not only of his uncle's influence, but also of the fortune Pyotr Shenshin had promised to leave his "unrecognized" nephew: the money turned out to have been embezzled. Despite these disappointments, Fet entered the army. He became an officer in a regiment of cuirassiers stationed deep in the Ukraine; as a result he was separated for many years from Moscow and the literary circle of which he had become a member. Of course it is true that even in the backwoods to which he was consigned Fet found individuals with whom he could conduct intellectual discourse. They were the Brzhevsky family, a young and cultivated landowner with poetic leanings and his gifted and attractive wife. Both ardent admirers of Fet's poetry, they appreciated his loneliness among the officers of his regiment and the provincial gentry, shared his literary interests, and—most important of all for Fet—listened to, and gave him their opinion of, his new poems. A thirst for friendship with people who understood art, literature, and music led Fet and the Brzhevskies eagerly to seek each other's company. It also led to Fet's introduction to, and love affair with, Mariya Lazich, the daughter of an impecunious landowner of that area. Yet Fet sacrificed this exceptional young girl for the sake of his career. Soon after he parted with her she died, a suspected suicide. Despite the tragedy of their relations, Fet never forgot Mariya and to the end of his life wrote poems inspired by her memory. His friendship for the Brzhevsky family was also a feeling he retained for many long years: the image of the landowner's wife appears in a number of his later poems. Undoubtedly, Fet's limited opportunities for forming friendships at that time, combined with a great burgeoning of his poetic talent, resulted in an intensification and deepening of his feeling for the few people he found congenial.

Fet added the poems written in the middle of the 1840's to those printed in journals of preceding years to form a new collection. It was approved by the censor in 1847, but lack of funds and the poet's absence from Moscow delayed its publication until 1850. This little book, with the modest title of *Stikhotvoreniia A. Feta* (*Poems by A. Fet*), was remarkable not only for the splendid new poems it added to those that had already won wide favor, but also, and perhaps chiefly, for presenting Fet for the first time as a poet of striking individuality.

The division of the book into sections and cycles, however, is not always convincing. Some poems, which in mood, imagery, and theme clearly belong to a definite cycle, are scattered throughout various sections. Notwithstanding its loose organization, the volume as a whole has inherent unity and distinction. Russia, with its patriarchal village life, its bleak, snow-covered plains, its troikas galloping recklessly into the distance with their young passengers laughing into the face of the snowstorm, its mystical Christmas season, its wooden towns aching with loneliness, its strange ballads reflecting so accurately the dramas of ordinary life—it is this Russia that emerges from the pages of Fet's poetry, whose originality is only emphasized by the imperishable beauty of the classical verse form. It is as if the poet were living in two worlds. He is captivated by the harmony of classical beauty on the one hand, and by foreign poetry. be it the ironic Romanticism of the young Heine or the intricate ornamentation of oriental forms, on the other. But above all he loves his native land, as mysterious as it is familiar to him, and finds inspiration in its vast and desolate wintry spaces, its pale Northern landscape. It was perhaps these contradictory emotions that led the poet, without his realizing it, to reject the traditional conception of beauty as an ideal lying outside of man's ordinary experience, an ideal developed during the golden age of classical art. Fet was keenly sensitive to the beauty of the world about him and looked upon beauty as an integral part of real life.

During the first twenty years of Fet's creative activity, his yearning toward the ideal, and at the same time his inner sense of dedication to, and identification with, the world about him, lent ambivalence to his poetry. In fact this ambivalence was its very essence. When the collection of 1850 appeared, Apollon Grigorev wrote: "Two aspects of Fet's poetry are clearly to be seen: ... we find brilliance and lucidity of expression in Fet's poems wrought in classical forms.... But Fet is also a subjective poet, and one who gives voice to the most poignant heartache of modern man."[4]

These two aspects coexisted in the poet's work, now one side dominating, now the other.

During a visit to Italy, Fet wrote:

> How have you lied to me, oh Italy!
> For long I cherished visions in my heart,
> But found the substance how unlike the dream!
> No kinship know I with your air.
> Upon your plains other and dearer scenes
> Arise and dwell in my imagination.
> Son of the North, I love the soughing wood,
> The dampy green of moss and foliation.... (90)

In this poem Fet declares he had held Italy to be the promised land, whose beauty was beyond anything hitherto conceived; but now, as he looks upon reality and not a dream, he realizes that beauty is one, whether it be the beauty of Italy or of his native land. The poem raised some eyebrows among those for whom the art of classical antiquity remained the standard for measuring all beauty and who therefore placed the highest value on the anthological poems in the collection. "Italy" was, accordingly, a poem of great significance insofar as it indicated the course that Fet's development as a poet was to take during the second half of the 1850's. But at the time the collection .appeared, the poet was far from anticipating his reevaluation of the classical ideal of the beautiful, even though the new poems of this "son of the North," who "gave voice to the most poignant heartache of modern man," patently triumphed over the translations from Greek and Latin included in the volume, as well as over his own poems in the classical manner. The lack of harmony and the tragic conflict that racked the soul of Fet's hero of those days, and the gloomy landscape of his descriptions, stand in eloquent contrast to the classical ideal of harmony and the traditional conception of beauty.

The very division of the collection of 1850 into sections and cycles reflects the relationship of the two tendencies and their significance for Fet at this stage in his development.

II *The Poet's Vision of His Native Land*

The beginning of the 1850 collection makes clear its connection with the "homeland" tendency. The title of the first cycle, "Snega" ("Snow"), takes the reader directly into the Russian landscape, whose characteristics make it the antithesis of the Graeco-Roman landscape, succulent and noonday, sung in classical verse.

The first poem of the first cycle speaks of Fet's appreciation of the melancholy beauty of the Northern scene, of his preference for it, and his awareness that it is an inextricable part of his love for his native land.

> I am a Russian, I love the silence of vast spaces
> Blanketed in snow, monotonous as death; the firs
> In tapering caps or silver-grey with hoarfrost;
> The river purling underneath blue panes of ice.
> With what delight my wandering gaze discovers
> Snow down-swept in gulleys, up-swept on hills;

Somnolent blades of grass; naked fields
Where midnight hours have raised a sculptured mound,
Like marble sepulchre, with far winds swirling
Above the solemn shine to sounds funereal. (691)

The depth of the poet's feeling and the full significance of
the emphasis on the first words of this first poem in the collection
become clear when we recall that his declaration "I am a
Russian ..." contradicts the facts. (In the application he submitted for admission to the university he had written, "I am
the son of foreigners," and above his signature, "To this document the foreigner Fet appends his signature.") This biographical detail gives the poem a double meaning: it reveals the
esthetic response of this "son of the North" to the somber land
of his birth, and at the same time it demonstrates that he was
indeed its true and devoted son and no foreigner in spirit.
Both meanings were of deep and vital importance to him. The
poem introduces his major theme and is closely linked with
the remainder of the poems in the collection. The poet's paradoxical vision of the world, nowhere more evident than in this
poem, was obvious to his readers. Undoubtedly it was this that
made Ivan Turgenev insist on Fet's revising the poem, straighten-
ing out its logic and thereby changing its entire poetic structure.

Contemporary students of Fet's work point out the contradictions in the poems of the "Snow" cycle and identify them
with basic qualities peculiar to all of his poetry. According to
Boris Bukhshtab, "Fet is concerned with registering the most
subtle shades of feeling—vague, undefined emotions."[5] Using
"Pechal'naia berioza" ("The Sorrowing Birch") from the "Snow"
cycle as his example, Bukhshtab shows how the poet combines
joy and sorrow, assertion and denial, love of life and love of
death.

The American critic Gustafson, disagreeing with Bukhshtab,
offers his own interpretation of the paradoxical juxtaposition of
joy and death in the "Snow" cycle. Seeing in these poems Fet's
realization of esthetic principles later formulated in his article
on Tyutchev, Gustafson maintains that the poet is interested in
only one aspect of a phenomenon—the esthetic. According to
this scholar, the world of beauty (the only world of importance

to Fet) lies beyond the objective categories of life and death; this approach enables him to combine things which would appear to be incompatible—joy and death.[6] Such an interpretation leaves unanswered the question of why the death motif should be woven into this particular cycle, dedicated to representations of the Russian landscape. It must also be said that Fet's conception of beauty was much broader than might be concluded from the formulations set forth in his article on Tyutchev and in assertions made in the heat of argument, when his opinions were coarsened and sharpened by his ardor.

The "Snow" cycle and others included in the collection of 1850 create an image of the poet's native land and of the inner world of one who is part of this land. At the same time they are a revelation of the conception of beauty held by Fet during that period.

It is true that themes of death and sorrow are interwoven with those of life and joy in the "Snow" cycle, but they are only one aspect of the poetic depiction of reality, with its manifold values and attributes.

The laconic quality of Fet's poetry and its wealth of associations at even so early a period of his writing can best be understood against the rich background of his literary heritage. Images, such as Pushkin's "inscrutable steppe" and Tyutchev's "eternal polar reaches," symbolizing the puissant northland that offers no answer to impassioned inquiries as to man's destiny— such images were familiar to readers of Pushkin and Gogol, Lermontov and Tyutchev.

Tyutchev introduces the image of "eternal polar reaches" as the antithesis to the fiery and, in his opinion, illusory dreams of the revolutionary Decembrists. Herzen follows this poetic tradition by writing, at the end of the 1850's, his "Growth of Revolutionary Ideas in Russia," a modern "Lives of the Saints" depicting Russian poets and thinkers who were unable to adapt themselves to "this frozen hell" and incapable of enduring "the piercing, unrelenting wind."[7] He cites the passage from Petrarch which Pushkin used as an epigraph to the sixth chapter of *Eugene Onegin,* in which Pushkin speaks of the incongruity of Lensky's death, a youth born for glory and perhaps even the benefit of mankind:

La, sotto i giorni nubilosi e brevi
Nasce una gente a cuil' morir non dole.

(There where the days are short and cloudy
Is born a tribe to whom death brings no grief.)

Similar associations underlie Fet's picture of the silent, deserted plain contemplated by a courageous youth deeply attached to his native land but fated to meet a tragic end there.

This poetic concept, which, as Fet later expressed it, "shines" through his pictures of the winter landscape—with nature in mourning, snowdrifts suggesting sepulchers, and the silence of night all around—does not yet supply the key to the paradox of the "Snow" poems, in which motifs of joy and death are closely linked. The reason for this commingling is that the hero of these poems—and, as naturally follows, the poet himself—is enchanted with the melancholy expanses of frozen wilderness and finds in them not only his ideal of beauty, but moral support as well. He is not the prisoner of this grim world, but the child of it, and one who is passionately devoted to it.

In this respect, the poems of the "Snow" cycle and especially the first of them, which introduces the 1850 collection as well, may be compared with Lermontov's famous "Rodina" ("Native Land") written not so much earlier:

I love my native land, but with a curious love
That mind and logic have no power to quell.
Not glory bought at price of blood,
Nor peace impregnate with a proud complacency,
Nor customs handed down from the dark past—
No, none of these stir pleasurable dreams.
And yet I love—just what, I cannot say:
Perhaps the frozen silence of her steppe,
The ceaseless surging of her boundless forests,
Rivers in spate that vie with shoreless seas . . .
I love to fly in peasant cart on country roads,
And, as my eyes explore the deepening shadows,
Descry the lights of one of her sad villages
Where I would find a harbor for the night.[8]

The blending of calculated coldness and majesty in the descriptions, the preference given to night and evening scenes, the reference to the impoverished lives of the peasants—all these elements of Lermontov's poem are found in Fet's "winter" cycles in the 1850 collection. The chief bond uniting the two poets is their love for their very real and austere native land. A structural likeness also exists between Fet's "I Am a Russian" and Lermontov's "Native Land." In both poems, scenes of their homeland are linked by the words "I love." In both, the scenes themselves show the movement of the author's thoughts: at first, the image of the country is conveyed by a broad panorama showing nature in its most typical aspect and mood; then the poet speaks of what his eye falls directly upon.

But while Lermontov discovers the distinguishing quality of his "curious love" by contrasting it with traditional forms of national pride—pride in the nation's glory bought with blood, pride in the country's past—Fet assesses the immediate scene by contrasting it with the classical definition of beauty as harmony.

It is of interest that the poignant love of native land and the ambivalence of this love experienced by both Fet and Lermontov at the beginning of the 1840's are expressed in the first volume of Gogol's *Dead Souls*, completed in 1842. Like Fet and Lermontov, Gogol expresses his love through descriptions of typical scenery: as he surveys the vast prospect unrolling before his eyes, "the immense fields," "the pine tips wrapped in mist," "ravens like clouds of flies, and any amount of horizon," he compares them with the luxurious scenery of "far lands and fair," and exclaims, addressing himself to Russia: "Everything about you is open, empty, even; nothing captivates and charms the eye. What is it, then, that so mysteriously and irresistibly draws one to you? . . . What promise is to be read in these limitless spaces?"[9]

The difference between Fet's portrayal of his native land and that of Lermontov and Gogol lies in Fet's more restricted view. Gogol took a bird's-eye view, as it were, of the vast Russian plain,[10] and Lermontov saw it as a traveler riding over its endless roads and fields, but Fet observed it all from a fixed point, his own home. His vision is bounded by the horizon. He notices changes in the inanimate winter scene because they occur in objects he knows intimately from daily observation.

"With what delight my wandering gaze discovers / Snow down-swept in gullies, up-swept on hills; ... naked fields / Where mid-night hours have raised a sculptured mound, / Like marble sepulchre, with far winds swirling" writes the poet, knowing well that the hills were bare and the gullies empty the day before, and no mound adorned the fields.

Fet is keenly aware of the world about him, and this world, with its peculiar moral atmosphere, represents for him his entire native land. The theme of melancholy love for his surround-ings and his spiritual kinship with them runs through cycle after cycle of the 1850 collection.

As mentioned above, the conception and structure of the first poem in the "Snow" cycle is determined by the phrase "I love." In the third poem we again find: "Dear God! How I love to see a troika come flying into view, as suddenly to vanish!" In the fifth poem of the cycle, "The Sorrowing Birch," the poet notes changes wrought in a single night to a tree he has ob-served from day to day. Here, too, we find the theme of love for, and kinship with, the world about him. ("I love the play of dawnlight on its boughs..."). The seventh poem begins directly with: "Oh lovely scene, how very dear!" Here, as in the third poem, a sleigh passes: "A distant sleigh on its lonely run...." Such images emphasize the static viewpoint of the writer, the limited space within which he makes his observations and through which the traveler passes.

The poet's house is the vantage point from which he observes the landscape. Often this is done through the window, as noted in these passages from the "Snow" cycle:

> A northern morning, sleepy, scrimpy,
> Casts a languid glance within.
>
> (third poem of the cycle)

> A sorrowing birch
> Stands by my window ....
>
> (fifth poem)

> Frost has made a pattern
> On the double panes....
>
> (ninth poem)

"Snow" is the only poem in which the troika is not a vision passing through the poet's limited world, but three horses and a sleigh waiting to take him on a journey. His own house is the point of departure:

> The night is bright, the frost is sharp,
> Come out into the creaking snow.

It is not a long journey that is anticipated, but a drive through familiar places. Despite the austerity of the scenery described in the "Snow" cycle, the poet finds it natural and essential that he should love it and feel that he is part of it.

The fourth poem of the cycle, presenting a winter scene with a troika dashing through the blizzard, has something of the mystery of a ballad. The rhythm of the poem was chosen to make it sound like a folk song.

> A mad wind, a bad wind, over the fields is
>   Galloping,
> Drifts of snow upon the steppe are
>   Quivering.
> The moonlit plain for miles around is
>   Glistening.
> With little bells the wind rings news of
>   Humankind.
> It shrieks beneath an oaken cross and
>   Vanishes.
> The steppeland hare is roving far and
>   Fearlessly.   (155–56)

Here, as in "I Am a Russian," we have a picture of the Northern winter with its snowdrifts ruffled by the wind and its fields swept by the blizzard.

Pushkin and Gogol saw the verst-posts (milestones) along the highway with the eyes of a traveler in a troika behind three galloping horses.

> Like palings the versts flash by,
> Distracting the idle eye.
>   (Pushkin, *Eugene Onegin*)

And before you know it, there you are counting the verst posts till your head goes round (Gogol, *Dead Souls*).

Fet sees such a post during a nocturnal ramble over the fields. It suddenly rises up in front of him, sparkling with frost. A troika dashes past, the wind carries back to his ears the jingle of its bells, informing him that the unknown traveler through this hinterland that is the poet's home has gone on his way past the endless series of verst posts, leaving the poet behind, standing beside the grave of one who, as a criminal or a suicide, has been deprived of decent burial in a graveyard.

The poem has a curious ending. The hare is not afraid of storm, or solitude, or this strange grave beside the road. Nor is it afraid of the poet standing there, nor of the "lifeless expanses." Both of them, the hare and the poet, are natives of this country—this is their own steppe. Such an analogy may seem preposterous to the rational minded, accustomed to drawing a sharp line between the human and animal worlds. But for Fet, who attributed the greatest importance to man's "natural" life and who devoted almost more space in his memoirs to recollections of dogs and horses than of human beings, this line of demarcation is very faint. Animals included in the "sphere" of the individual are an indivisible part of the individual's life. One senses this in his poem "Derevnia" ("The Village"), included among the "Miscellany" of the 1850 collection. In composition it resembles "Snow":

> I love the warmth and the sadness
> Of your home in that village remote;
> The chimes floating over the greenwood,
> Golden cupolas crowned by a cross;
>
> I love the untrodden meadow,
> The mist creeping up to the door,
> The intimate circle that gathers
> At dusk round the samovar;
>
> I love the bespectacled granny
> In her lacy, beribboned cap,
> The golden glow of the kernels
> Of oats on plates on the sill;

And on an occasional table,
A basket spilling a sock;
The frisky tabby cat leaping
At a ball of wool on the floor;

The granddaughter, quiet and wistful,
In the prettiest possible frock,
Pale hands with beautiful motions,
Modestly lowered lids. . . .

Tales of my own invention,
Cool air out of evening skies,
And of all rewards, the highest—
A glance from her wondering eyes. (255)

Again we have anaphora, the phrase "I love" serving as a
connecting link, but here the reason for the poet's love is quite
different from that in "Snow": here he loves life in the village
because it is the sphere in which the girl he loves moves. His
vision first sweeps to the horizon, then narrows to take in the
village house, narrows still more to focus upon the group around
the tea table.[11] The poet is enamored of the people and scenery surrounding his beloved, the sounds she hears, the light that
plays upon her, the woods and meadows she visits, the house
she lives in. He loves the cat that gambols at her feet and the
knitting she holds in her hands.

All of this represents her. The list of things filling her "life
sphere," the furnishings of the house, the attributes of the
landscape, should not be regarded as haphazard, unrelated objects. They form a vital and organic whole. The girl herself is
the soul of this little world, an inseparable part of her family,
home, and village. Within this circle there is no hierarchy of
things—all are equally dear and important to him. The gold cross
crowning the cupola at the edge of this world and the plate of
golden oats on the windowsill inside the house are equated,
despite the great disparity in their functions.

The rising moon, pale phantom,
The farewells of bedding birds,
The shimmer of china teacups,
The dying down of our talk.

One's attention is invariably drawn to the parallelism of imagery: the hushing of the birds, the subsiding of the conversation; the rising of the moon, the shimmer of the teacups. All are intimately related, equally loved and equally significant. By entering this "life sphere," the poet himself becomes part of it and in this new environment assumes a new attitude toward himself. He loves himself as part of this circle, loves the stories he invents and which become identified with the atmosphere surrounding the "quiet" and "bashful" granddaughter and bring him into contact with the center of this circle: her eyes and her inner world. A sense of the closeness, the exclusiveness of this world is conveyed by his perceiving mostly round objects in the house—the table, the samovar, the cups, the plates of oats, the old lady's spectacles, the ball of wool on the floor.

The poem "The Village" has a compositional distinction of the greatest importance for the poet's future development. It is written in the first person, and this person is highly lyrical. He reiterates the phrase "I love." His love, however, is itself an expression of his relationship to the world about him, in this case a village world, and so it might be reduced to a single adjectival qualification: his "beloved" world. He portrays it as a space filled with objects bathed in his love. In other words, one detects a tendency to transform the lyric into one of those verbless word pictures with which Fet was destined to astonish and delight his readers (even the most exacting lovers of poetry) in later years. One such lyric ("A whisper, a faintest breath...") found its way into the 1850 collection; another, written in the 1880's, resembles "The Village" in that the enumeration of objects, feelings, changes in nature, expresses in its sum a single idea: Spring. In "The Village," the concluding chord struck is: She.

Another characteristic that establishes an affinity between "The Village" and Fet's "verbless" lyrics is that of movement within the poem. We have already noted that Fet's gaze travels from the wider to the more intimate scene, seeing all things in their relationship to the center. The poem concentrates upon a definite "life sphere"; this remains the principal poetic image. But the poet presents this sphere in time. It is not merely "the village," but the village in the evening, from the ringing of

vespers to the rising of the moon, an interval of time sufficient
for the ceremony of tea drinking, the telling of tales of the
poet's own invention, the exhausting of most topics of conversation, and the final achievement of the poet's purpose, which is
to make the lovely granddaughter lift her shy gaze to his face.
Here, the parallelism of imagery—the subsiding of the birds'
chatter and the waning of conversation, the light of the moon,
and the shimmer of the teacups in this light—has the dual purpose of showing that these phenomena, "side by side" in space
(appertaining to her "sphere"), are also side by side in time.

In its artistic conception as well as in its manner of portraying the beauty of secluded village life, Fet's poem has much
in common with those chapters from Pushkin's *Eugene Onegin*
depicting the rural scene.

As an epigraph to the second chapter, Pushkin uses Horace's
exclamation "O rus!..." and adds to it his own "O Rus!" Super-
ficially, this would seem to be a translation, whereas Horace's
"O rus!" means "O country life!" and Pushkin's "Rus" is the
ancient name of Russia. The combination of the two is, then,
a play on words, suggesting that the Russia of Pushkin's time
was to be identified with country or village life, with its customs and traditions, its scenery, its rustic inhabitants.

The elder daughter, Tatyana, heroine of Pushkin's poem, was
the very soul of the countryside where the Larins' manor house
was situated. When, in later years, Onegin recalled his visit to
them, he always envisioned "the manor house with her at the
window . . . always alone." Pushkin asserts that the very name
"Tatyana" evokes "the memory of ancient times or serving maids'
quarters." Tatyana's true nature, so akin to that of the simple
folk, fostered as it was by the patriarchal mores of country life,
is revealed during the Yuletide festivities: "Tatyana believed in
the lore of simple folk handed down from time immemorial:
in dreams, cartomancy, prognostications by the moon." Lensky,
another character from the poem, had good reason to compare
her with Svetlana as fortune-teller from Zhukovsky's well-known
ballad of the same name.

Fet's treatment of the Russian village was similar to Pushkin's; for both poets, it was a major theme.

Folklore, an integral part of the old patriarchal way of life,

finds its place in the two cycles "Snow" and "Fortune-telling."
The women in these cycles are of the world of snow and storm.

Not only in his narrative poem *Eugene Onegin* but in many
of his lyrics, Pushkin paints portraits of Russian girls whose
lives are lived close to nature and who are raised in the traditions of the ancient village. In "Winter. What Is There to Do
in the Village?" he describes a nocturnal rendezvous:

> A maid at twilight comes out on the porch,
> Bared her throat, her breast, the wind full in her face.
> But the northern blast cannot blight the Russian rose,
> Like a passionate kiss does she flame in the frost.
> How fresh the Russian maid in the snow![12]

In Fet's "I know, my pretty one, you fear not the moonlit
night . . ." (from the "Snow" cycle) this theme is repeated, but
with greater mystery: the poet does not tell us whether it is
love or the contemplation of the winter night that impels the
girl to leave her bed. But the closing lines, using an idea borrowed from folk songs, intimate that it is love. Russian folk
songs often speak of the snowstorm that separates lovers by
burying all the roads and paths. This is how Fet employs the
theme:

> But ah, my pretty! I do fear
> The evil spirit of the night
> Will raise a storm and cover up
> The path your feet have worn. (155)

On Twelfth night eve it was customary for young girls to
appeal to this fearful "spirit of the night" to tell them their fate.
To this tradition Fet's "Fortune-telling" cycle is devoted. If in
Pushkin's *Eugene Onegin* and Zhukovsky's ballads this custom
is treated with the light irony of detachment—though with full
appreciation of the charm of this quaint superstition—Fet speaks
as one participating in the fortune-telling. The fear and awe
expressed in the verse are enhanced by the girl's longing for
happiness. In the fifth and last poem of the cycle, the poet
becomes the "oracle" in this "testing of fate." He hears the girl

asking a passing stranger his name in the hope it will be the same as the name mentioned when her fortune was told. Pushkin portrays a similar scene with gay humor:

> Hark! Crunching snow. A wayfarer! The maid
>   On tiptoe to him flies,
> And sweeter than the shepherd's pipe
>   The voice that greets his ear:
> "What is your name?" He scans her face
>   Before replying, "Agafon."[13]

This night scene becomes more mysterious and folk-like in Fet's treatment. Out of the darkness comes a sleigh bearing a stranger who speaks his name, and this name is the same as that cited by the fortune-teller.

> Someone glides through the shadows,
>   A sleigh is flying past;
> A voice rings out in the darkness:
>   "Tell me, sir, your name!" . . .
> Like the voice of Fate the answer,
>   Taking her unawares;
> Her quilted jacket rises
>   With a sudden catching of breath.[14]
>
> (166 and 693)

III *Melodies*

The first poem of the next cycle, "Melodies," announces like an arresting chord the transition to a new key. Not only is the key changed, the whole system of visual images is changed as well.

> Pearls of the orient—her teeth;
> Shemakhansky silk—her hair;
> As soft and bright as a morning in spring
>   Is the shine of her almond eyes. (408)

Here we have oriental splendor, Southern languor, fierce and passionate love—a world of exotic beauty, a far cry from the

sad and pensive beauty of the Russian village buried in snow
or gently awakening in the spring.

The beloved in these poems is compared to a diamond
sparkling in the moonlight (second poem of the cycle), her eyes
to the stars. She herself appears to the poet, "a tambourine in
her hands, rapture in her eyes" (eleventh poem); again he sees
her as an Italian signora (fifteenth poem), or as one whom he
comes upon in an arbor hung with grapes and dappled by the
Southern sun (sixteenth poem).

The mysteriousness of this love differs from that of the preceding two cycles. It belongs wholly to the world of poetry:
it is fashioned of only the beautiful and the harmonious, and
it is traditional in its associations and images. The very music of
the verse is that of the medieval romance and reminds us of
minstrels' lays:

> I will know you at once, in your snow-white veil,
> Where the sweet-smelling almond tree scatters its blooms,
> Glimpsed from the saddle, or over garden wall,
> In the light of the moon or the blaze of the sun;
> And from far away I hear your guitar,
> Above ripple of fountain and nightingale's song. . . .
>
> (410)

A break occurs in the "Melodies" after the fifteenth poem: the
numbering begins over again and proceeds from one to twenty.
This break is not noted in the index, which numbers the poems
in succession up to thirty-five. But a definite change in the
style of the cycle can be remarked after the fifteenth poem.
In the sixteenth (No. 1 of the second series) the poet once more
speaks as a thoughtful, ironic man of the 1840's, torn by inner
contradictions. Thus Dr. Faustus cruelly interrupts the avowals
of the woman who loves him by declaring with bitter cynicism:

> How much trust in those eyes! I do earnestly say
> No lovelier friend could I find.
> But why this deceit? Let us say what we wish;
> Have we need of these cautious conceits?
> A yawning gulf, my dear, divides
> Your joy everlasting from mine. (434)

The poem "Polunochnye obrazy" ("Midnight Visions") is written in a similar vein and reminds us, in theme, of Goethe's dedication to *Faust*, which Fet translated and included in the 1850 collection.

> Midnight visions are howling
> Like spirits that frighten the dog;
> I dread to hear them inform me,
> It was I who summoned them here.[15]

Tragic as Goethe's dedication is, we find a sad resignation in its mood that is lacking in "Midnight Visions," whose tone is more in accord with the first scenes of *Faust*. Apollon Grigorev used the imagery of Fet's poem to illustrate the qualities peculiar to the heroes of "morbid poetry" in general.

"We must not forget," he wrote, "that these phantoms, summoned by a sickly, supersensitive ego, punish him who summons them, pursuing him relentlessly as they pursued Manfred, giving him not a moment's peace." In the same article, Grigorev compares the persona of such poems to Hamlet.[16]

Fet's translation of Goethe's dedication to *Faust* is, in its turn, dedicated to A. G., i.e., to Apollon Grigorev. His *Faust* poems, like his *Hamlet* ones (the cycles "To Ophelia" and "Melancholy"), were written at the time when he was living with Apollon Grigorev in Moscow and shared his moods and spiritual searchings with him. In the article cited above, written in 1853, Grigorev asserts that the cycles "Melodies," "To Ophelia," and "Melancholy" belong to the "morbid tendency" in Fet's poetry.[17]

In the cycle "To Ophelia" Fet voices the sentiments of a morose, disappointed man of his day, a man "sick" with the moral ailments of his epoch and in love with a delicate, impulsive creature imbued with sorrow and doomed to destruction. The heroine of this cycle has nothing in common with the poet's beloved in the first half of "Melodies," but much in common with the woman who emerges in the second half. She is a shy and selfless creature who suffers the humiliation of hearing her Hamlet address such words to her as:

> How becoming is that pallor,
> Eloquent that silent grief,
> And that poverty of spirit—
> Ah, I pity you indeed! (444)

At other times, he worships at her feet and confesses that his proud spirit and poetic genius are utterly dependent upon her who, however humble and innocent, is possessed of a nature rich in its very simplicity.

> As fair are you, my beloved,
> As a blue-eyed Zephyr òf May,
> And as sensitive my spirit
> As a golden Aeolian harp.
>
> Under the touch of live feelings
> Its strings, though they be but few,
> Find harmonies new to capture
> Every new breath of your soul. (403)

The sorrowful and ephemeral Ophelia presents a stark contrast to the heroines of the cycle "In Imitation of Oriental Poetry," the last poem of which, "Wonder Not That I Am Dark," derives its inspiration from "The Song of Songs."

> Wonder not that I am dark,
> Scorched to darkness by the sun,
> But admire my grace of form
> As I move among my sisters. . . .
>
> Call me now your mountain rose,
> By my beauty you are pricked,
> I'm a love-flower born to bloom
> In the chamber where you lie. (126)

Ophelia is frail and incorporeal. She is a fusion of joy and sorrow, so much "the ideal" that she might be but "an airy vision" conjured up by the poet's incantation. The second poem of the cycle "Ne zdes' li ty legkoiu ten'iu" ("Was It Not Here Your Pale Shadow . . .") sounds like an echo of the dedication

to *Faust*. Even Ophelia's death is but a beautiful, if melancholy,
diversion for the poet and is not Ophelia herself but a figment
of the poet's (Hamlet's) imagination?

> Ophelia sang as she perished
> And wove a wreath as she sang;
> With flowers and wreath and with singing,
> To the bed of the river she sank.
>
> And much with her singing descended
> To the darkest bed of my soul,
> For much have I of singing,
> And feeling and dreaming and tears.   (133)

The closing lines clearly identify Hamlet's beloved with the
poet. Ophelia sinks to the dark depths of his soul along with
his dreams. Thus, the river in which the drowned Ophelia floats,
and Ophelia herself, represent in metaphor the hopes and sufferings of the poet. This subjective perception of the world
about him presents an objective image of the suffering egoist,
Hamlet, the hero of the cycle. Yet there is another facet to
Ophelia's character, as expressed in these poems. Despite her
frailty and vulnerability, she is capable of offering moral support
to others. In unburdening his heart to her, Hamlet reveals an
awareness of the kinship of their suffering. The imagery of her
songs strikes an answering note in his heart. She sings of a
lonely grave; this image has associations with Fet's memories
of friends for whom it "was not hard to perish" beneath "this
gloomy sky" (the fourth poem of the "Snow" cycle, which men-
tions the lonely grave beside the road); she sings of the willow,
which symbolized for the poet his melancholy, Northern homeland and his lonely, grieving spirit. The song of the willow
is the song of Desdemona, the strong and loving wife of a great
man who ruined himself as well as the woman he loved. Ophelia,
who repeats this song, may be said to be a worthy sister of
Desdemona. This is Desdemona's song:

> I am ill, Ophelia, my sweetest friend,
>   My heart and my eye are grown feeble;
> Oh, sing me a song of the wind that blows
>   O'er the mound where my love lies lonely.

The suffering soul and the sickly breast
Understand my sighing and moaning.
Oh, sing me a song of the willow green,
A song for your own Desdemona! (132)

In the next poem, Ophelia is not so much the victim of the suffering egoist as his friend and support. It is to her alone that he turns for help; it is only in her and in her love that he believes:

Pray with all your tender heart
For yourself, and yet for me.

Exorcize with words of love
The doubts assailing me.
Let my troubled soul find peace
Beneath the quiet wings of prayer. (133)

Among his "doubts" was the poet's atheism, which, as we know, soon grew into a firm conviction. In asking her to "Pray . . . for yourself and yet for me," the poet indicates his own inability to believe in the power of prayer. But while he does not believe in Divine help, neither does he believe in the saving power of reason. All these qualities of mind are expressed through the image of Hamlet—a figure of world literature congenial to the Russian mind and adopted by Russian literature.

The cycle "To Ophelia" owes its distinction to the original interpretation by the poet of Shakespeare's Hamlet and Ophelia, and the intensity with which the younger poet relives his predecessor's masterpiece, becoming, as it were, co-author, with his own conception of characters and situations, his own psychological attributes conferred upon the hero.

Fet's own atheism is fundamental to Hamlet's request that Ophelia pray for him, and Hamlet's pessimistic social and historical outlook becomes the pessimism of the disillusioned thinkers of the 1840's.

IV *Philosophical Bases of the Collection of 1850*

In the 1850 collection we find a reflection of Fet's philosophical inquiries, his thoughts on the meaning of life, his skepticism, his dissatisfaction with theoretical solutions of the problems confronting the individual. For Fet, the individual represented the point of departure of any philosophical system. The individual, the significance of his existence, his longing for the infinite and his physical finiteness, his reason and his instincts—these were matters of primary importance to Fet. He pursued their study throughout his life, and his first views are intimated in the poems of the 1840's. The final link in the chain of his philosophical reflections appears in the works of the 1870's and 1880's; the poems of these years are the poetic embodiment of his conclusions.

No such answers to philosophical problems are offered in the 1840's and 1850's, because at that time he gave preference to an instinctive penetration of the secret of life's essence through poetic perception.

Fet's antirationalism and rejection of hard, logical answers to the basic problems of philosophy, as well as his social pessimism, find expression in this collection (and indeed in all of his creative work of the 1840's) in his choice of subject matter, which utterly excludes anything of a social or political nature. It is clear that even so early he looked upon art as a refuge from the evils of social reality, as an intellectual atmosphere devoted solely to the contemplation of the highest and most generalized questions of human existence. Among these he did not include problems of social progress, for he appears not to have believed in such progress. His skeptical attitude seems to have been formed in his student days when, in the midst of a sudden outburst of enthusiasm for Georg Wilhelm Friedrich Hegel's philosophy, he stood apart from his friends and worked out his own answers to basic problems. There is reason to believe that at this time he first read Schelling. He assigned great importance to his having made the acquaintance, at the beginning of the 1840's, of Professor Shevyrov of Moscow University, and to the discussions he had with him. Shevyrov was an ardent admirer of Friedrich Schelling's philosophy, which, as it denied the idea of progress in the direct historico-social aspect of Hegel's treatment, might very well have played an important role in the formation of Fet's views.

The end of the 1840's was a time of political reaction following the revolution of 1848 in France. The chief blows stemming from this reaction were aimed at the Russian intelligentsia, especially writers, and consequently the rejection of political and social themes in poetry might be seen as a means of self-protection. Nikolay Nekrasov, who from the very beginning of his career as a poet made social problems the main theme of his creative work and identified himself with the radical wing of the Russian intelligentsia, noted the sharp decrease in interest in poetry at the end of the 1840's and the beginning of the 1850's.

In 1849, Nekrasov began his article "Russkie vtorostepennye poety" ("Russian Minor Poets") with the words: "There is no poetry." The disappearance of poetry from the pages of literary journals and the few collections of poetry published were noted by many critics of that day. On more than one occasion, Nekrasov remarked that in times of political reaction poetry was silent. (See his poems "Strashnyi god" ["The Dreadful Year"] and "Poetu" ["To the Poet"].)

In the 1860's Fet's skepticism grew into open and even aggressive antagonism toward groups struggling for social progress, into hatred for "theoreticians" who asserted that reason was the principal force making for the happiness of mankind in general and the individual in particular.

While a direct portrayal of all civic feeling is excluded from the collection of 1850, through a complicated series of associations some of the cycles and many of the poems indirectly express feelings and ideas born of the times, and reflect the attitude of people of the 1840's who recognized that they were children of their epoch. Apollon Grigorev was therefore fully justified in placing Fet's poetry alongside that of Heine and the revolutionary Russian poet Nikolay Ogarev; for the same reason, themes akin to those of Lermontov's lyrics (the native land theme, for instance) are found in Fet's poems of the 1840's. The lyrical tone of "Melancholy," reflecting the state of dissatisfaction, depression, creative and spiritual crisis characteristic of Fet's poetry of the 1840's, was equally typical of Nekrasov's poetry. In the latter's long poem "Poet i grazhdanin" ("Poet and Citizen"), he shows that in a period of political reaction a poet cannot be other than melancholy.

In contrast to Lermontov and Ogarev, to say nothing of Nekrasov, in those years Fet permitted only the vaguest suggestion of an idea to glimmer behind the portrait he drew of any individual. In the poems of 1850, his disbelief in the logic of feelings and his skepticism as to the possibility of direct and complete self-expression were perhaps his sole convictions as a poet, and ones that he openly declared. Yet Fet did not share the dire and tragic sense of inability to communicate expressed by Tyutchev in his "Silentium":

> Silence. Hide and disguise
> Your feelings and your dreams.
> Enough that in the soul's depths
> They rise and noiseless move
> Like stars in the night sky.
> Commune with them—in silence.[18]

Fet's sense of "insufficiency" of verbal expression and logical speech sprang from his profound need for complete spiritual communion with others. Accordingly, he sought and found other means of conveying thoughts and feelings, and delighted in these other means. The most powerful of these "tongues" was sound, especially the sound of music, which Fet felt could say so much, and with unmatched force and directness. In the collection of 1850, music is a theme encountered again and again. In one of his poems Fet contrasts the richness of the musical idiom with the limitations of logical speech:

> Heavy is my heart with the secret
> Communed by the dying violins.
> 'Mid the noise of this alien crowd
> Their message is doubly clear.
> With magic power they remind me
> Of all that I hold most dear.   (176)

In another one, called "Melody," he says:

> Like a cloud of tiny insects
> The winged sounds are fluttering. . . .
> Oh, that the soul could speak
> Without the intercession of words!   (177)

This same longing for communication and understanding and this same sense of the insufficiency of speech are found in his famous quatrain:

> Share your living dreams,
> Speak to this listening heart;
> Pour into my soul in sound
> What cannot be said in words.   (447)

But music is not the only "idiom" Fet adds to the media of human communication. We have already mentioned that he attributes to every individual a moral and material sphere uniquely his own. The objects surrounding the individual bear witness to that individual's nature. While awaiting his love in a garden, the poet is informed of her approach by the fragrance of the flowers. In the section devoted to imitations of eastern verse, Fet has a poem called "Iazyk tsvetov" ("The Language of Flowers"):

> How long have I been eager
> To commune in fragrant rhymes.
> Every blossom exhales a hint—
> Informs you of my confession;
> Perhaps the whole bouquet
> Will show the way to a tryst.   (444)

It is well known that oriental poets attribute meaning to the odors of various flowers and have created symbols for these meanings. Fet was captivated by the notion that the fragrance of flowers could be reduced to a language. He also wrote the poem "Khot' nel'zia govorit'" ("Though I Dare Not Speak"), in which he expresses the thought that, unspeaking and unseeing, lovers can communicate their thoughts through the fragrance of flowers.[19]

Together with poems about the language of music, objects, and odors, Fet has written about the language of glances, which are also deeply eloquent:

> Soon our span of years runs out,
> But within the given circle,

> Our eyes forever can commune,
> Dwell forever on each other.   (422)

According to the poet, no words are needed to supplement the message of a glance or the response to this message in the other's gaze.

Fet's eagerness to supplement verbal language with other forms of expression reveals, on the one hand, his lack of confidence in reason and rationalism, and, on the other, his attachment to natural, physical life in all its manifestations. In the end it was his antirational tendencies that led him to assert the irrational, intuitive nature of art, making art the most profound and all-embracing means by which man perceives and comprehends the world. This was the seed from which grew the theory of "pure art" in the form which Fet accepted.

Turgenev, who rejected Fet's principles, wrote him a letter obviously referring to a discussion they had already held: "You condemn the mind to ostracism and see in a work of art only the unconscious murmurings of one asleep." He accompanied this with a humorous drawing.[20]

The concept of sleep as a state in which the mind is absolutely tranquil and outside the realm of reason, a state in which it thoroughly and unconsciously unites with nature and culls new strength from this merging, is found as an original theme in Fet's poetry. In the 1850 edition, it appeared as new wine poured into the old bottle of the serenade form. Rejecting the usual theme of a morning serenade, which was the calling of the beloved to awaken, Fet, on the contrary, warns others not to wake her. His famous "Na zare ty ee ne budi" ("Do Not Wake Her at Dawn"), which in form and certain other respects reminds us of Pushkin's "Zimnee utro" ("Winter Morning"), might have been written as a deliberate answer to Pushkin, and reveals Fet's attitude toward sleep.

Pushkin wrote:

> It's time, my lovely one, awake!
> Open those eyes with languor heavy
> To meet our northland's bright Aurora!
> Arise, a splendid Northern star!

Last night a snowstorm raged, remember?
Dark veils were drawn upon a darker sky;
The moon, a sickly yellow disc,
Shone wanly through the scudding clouds,
And you disconsolately sat. . . .[21]

This is followed by a description of the glorious winter morning.

Fet's version is:

Do not wake her at dawn, I pray,
So sweetly she slumbers at dawn,
With the breath of the morn on her breast,
And the flush of the sun on her cheek. . . .

Last evening for long did she sit
At the window and endlessly gaze
At the frolicsome clouds in the sky
That caught at the moon as they passed;

And the brighter the light of the moon,
And the louder the nightingale's song,
The whiter the face at the pane,
And the sharper the ache of her heart.   (135)

As we see, Pushkin's prescription for overcoming the gloom of the evening is to meet the buoyant life of the new day, whereas Fet's is to lose oneself in unconsciousness, in the deep peace of sleep.

In the following verse, Fet subtly depicts sleep as the blending of man with nature:

Sleep. The summer dawn
Is yet too young and chill;
The stars above the hill
Shimmer through rising mists,

And but a moment past
The cocks gave third salute.
From yonder belfry float
Soft matutinal chimes;

> The summits of the limes
> Are bathed in languor sweet,
> The corners of your pillow
> Are damp with cooling dews.   (177)

The unity of man and nature during sleep is suggested by noting the poetic affinity of the sounds with which they both herald the coming of the new day (the crowing of the cocks, the chiming of the bells). The woman in the poem appears to be sleeping outdoors, an element adding solemnity and significance to the moment of her awakening. The tips of the lime trees and the sleeper's pillow seem to exchange functions: it is not the pillow, warmed by the human body, that breathes an air of languor, but the tips of the limes; and it is not the limes that give off the cooling moisture of early morning, but the corners of the pillow.

Even when the poet seems to betray his usual principle, by beginning with: "Come, awake!..." his voice fails him and he ends his morning serenade, awed to silence by the sanctity of sleep.

It is a curious fact that in a later collection of Fet's poetry, edited by Turgenev, Fet changed the ending of his poem, eliminating—evidently at the insistence of the editor—the lines showing his irrational reverence for sleep, amounting almost to deification.

Fet did not, however, relinquish his conception of sleep as a moment of fullest living, of acquiring physical and spiritual strength. Among his poems based on classical models and mythical subjects, he has one dedicated to "Sleep and Death," children of the Sun (Helios) and of Night. Of Sleep he says:

> Swarthy like his mother, born to create
> like his all-seeing father,
> Sleep, though encompassed by darkness, is
> mindful of daylight splendor.   (239)

He sees sleep as a source of creative energy to be expended in the daytime, this being sleep's high purpose:

> Perhaps the dreamer
> Will rouse from golden sleep;

> Or perhaps sweet verse
> Will flow from his parted lips.   (435)

That is why his "Ia prishol k tebe s privetom" ("I Come to You with a Greeting") may best be called a "morning serenade." In it, he expresses with particular forcefulness the idea that the hour of waking is the hour when man and nature are surcharged with creative energy.

This work, among the most popular of Fet's poems, is accepted by most readers as a "love" or "nature" poem (it is classified as the latter in children's readers). But many, including Turgenev and the eminent satirist and political writer Mikhail Saltykov-Shchedrin, regarded it as a poem about the artist and his work. Some see in it a declaration of the unconsciousness and unpurposefulness of creative effort (the poet sings as does a bird); others think it an exposition of the psychological state of the artist at the moment of inspiration.

V   *Nature Poetry*

Man, nature and their mutual interaction—this is the main theme of Fet's poetry. It provides noble situations, worthy, according to Fet, of being the source of poetic inspiration. Later he would declare it was the *only* subject worthy of a true poet. He maintained that the poetic gift manifests itself in heightened powers of observation, in the ability to see and reveal in the moods of both man and nature things hitherto unseen or, at least, unrecognized. By seeing things in a new way and presenting them in fresh imagery, poetry discovers anew the eternal attributes of nature.

In a poem dedicated to Fet, Tyutchev wrote:

> There are happy ones endowed by nature
> With instinct prophetic and blind.
> With this they hear, they see, the waters
> In the darkest depths of earth.
>
> Favorite child of the great mother,
> Oh, more than enviable your lot!
> For you have glimpsed her secret face
> Beneath the world's coarse carapace.[22]

Fet held the chief attribute of nature, one reflecting its very essence, to be its endless extension in time and space. The immortality of nature lay in its ceaseless change and uninterrupted flow. He compared the constant movement within the external world to the constant flow of impressions received and appraised by the human mind. It was the relationship of these two unceasing tides that formed the basis of his nature portrayal. But movement in nature, if ceaseless, is also pulsating. The flow of time is divided into moments, each of which is fleeting but not at all equal in content, and hence in value, to all others.

In "I Come to You with a Greeting," Fet's description of the morning is based upon two interrelated processes. He describes the break of day by enumerating some of the concomitant changes in nature; the recollection of the objective impressions he received while walking through the awakening forest evokes in him the same feelings they evoked at the time. It is these feelings that are captured in the poem:

> I come to you with a greeting,
> To tell you the sun has arisen,
> And has set the leaves aflutter
> With the warmth of its golden streaming;
>
> To tell you the woods have awakened,
> Awakened entire, every branch,
> And the birds have shaken their feathers
> And are filled with the spring's desire.
>
> I've come as I came last evening,
> To tell you with words as impassioned,
> I am ready and eager to serve you,
> And happiness serve forever. . . .
>
> Though I cannot yet say what the song
> Will be, I feel it within me growing.   (254)

The coming of morning is described in a series of events succeeding one another and depending on one another (the rising of the sun, the stirring of the forest, the awakening of the birds). The poet, too, passes through a series of moods. Fresh and buoyant after his night's rest, he moves from a contemplation of the agitated life about him to a sharing of its agitation and a feeling of oneness with his surroundings. In this ebullience of morning life he finds love and the creative impulse, two states of mind that lead, according to the poet, to the full unfolding of individuality. At the same time, the break of day is presented as an impulse to achieve something, a release of energy but not its realization. It is the moment of genesis, the beginning, the crossing of the threshold. But the processes taking place in nature and in man are not carried to fulfillment; the poet's voice breaks off before he can say what the song germinating within him is to be.

That this poem is in the nature of an improvisation has been noted by Gustafson, who has stressed the spontaneousness of the feelings captured at their inception and carried through their early stage of development. Boris Eikhenbaum, the Soviet critic, has made a thorough rhythmic and structural analysis of the poem and draws our attention particularly to the emotional significance of the enjambment, "Though I know not what the song / Will be. . . ." This has been done by others who have translated the poem into various languages.[23]

We shall see that in later years the portrayal of a "beginning" became a favorite subject with Fet. In this connection, let us analyze the use of this motif in a nature lyric—a poem in which his peculiar approach to natural phenomena is evident:

"Vesennii dozhd'" ("Spring Rain," 1859), despite its title, does not describe the shower itself but only its approach and the moment when it begins, as observed from a window.

> The sun still shines through rifts of cloud
> And all is bright beyond the window;
> A sparrow bathing in the sand
> Pecks at its breast with wings aflutter.   (139)

Suddenly the observer sees sheets of rain in the distance and watches their movement:

> But now from dome of heaven to earth
> Soft undulating veils are moving,

> And seen through them the distant wood
> Seems all in golden dust enveloped.   (139–40)

The "range of vision" is distinctly defined—it is bound by the woods at the horizon; the rain moves between woods and garden, bearing down on the house.

> Two drops come splashing on the pane,
> The limes give off a smell of honey,
> And into the garden something strides
> And drums on leaves of trees and bushes.   (140)

The observer's powers of recognition lag behind his sensual impressions. He is aware of the sharpening of odors, he sees the drops and hears their impact, but as yet refers to the rain as merely "something." The next moment he can say it is rain that has struck the house, but the poem ends before the action is complete and before its full meaning has been grasped.

In "Shopot" ("Whispers") Fet reveals his remarkable sense of movement in nature:

> Whispers, timid breathing,
>   The trilling of a nightingale,
> The silver and the heaving
>   Of a brook in the vale.
>
> Nocturnal light, nocturnal shadows,
>   Shadows in shadowy space,
> A play of wondrous changes
>   On the beloved face.
>
> In smoky clouds the red of roses
>   Where the day is born,
> And healing tears and kisses—
>   And the dawn, the dawn!   (211)

The first thing one notices (something instantly remarked by the poem's first readers) is the absence of verbs—a device which was adopted by the poet to emphasize movement in this picture of the nocturnal landscape and human emotions. He presents night as one significant moment after another, a stream of events. The poem tells us that night is followed by dawn, and that the lovers' quarrel is followed by the coming of the light. The movement in nature and the movement of human emotions parallel each other. This parallelism in the portrayal of man and nature as a distinctive feature of Fet's poetry has been noted by a number of scholars, among them Eikhenbaum, Bukhshtab and Pavel Gromov. In the case under consideration parallelism is basic to the structure of the poem. The precision and sheer nakedness of the composition, as well as the descriptive method of "spotting" the most significant details, have enabled the poet to press a world of content into an incredibly small space. Since, in poems not written in the classical style, Fet assigned greater importance to the kinesthetic and dynamic aspect of an object than to its form, he selected a few striking details as the means of conjuring up the entire picture rather than creating it by extensive description. He stimulates the reader's imagination by leaving much unsaid, and by enveloping what *is* said in veils of mystery. What is omitted has little importance for him. Action develops in "pulsations," and the poet merely marks those meaningful moments when changes occur in man and nature.

Here, then, is the "stream of events" of first importance in portraying the love scene suggested by this poem:

1. "Whispers. Timid breathing."—persuasion, explanation, and the response: vacillation, fear, timidity.

2. "A play of wondrous changes / On the beloved face."—night shadows playing over her face, but also changes of expression attending her change of mood.

3. "And healing tears and kisses / And the dawn, the dawn!"—exchanges end in the triumph of love; the two begin a new life.

Here is the "stream of events" in nature, a secondary succession:

1. "The trilling of a nightingale, / The silver and the heaving / Of a brook in the vale. / Nocturnal light, nocturnal shadows, / Shadows in shadowy space,"—this presents the night scene.

2. "In smoky clouds the red of roses / Where the day is born"—the "red of roses" suggests the first rays of sun.

3. "And the dawn, the dawn!"—the night is over.

In the final line of the poem the two streams merge. This ending on "a new intake of breath," so to speak, is more like the beginning than the ending of a poem, but this treatment was also characteristic of Fet, who saw in any mood, in any scene, a fragment of an endless process. And so this poem, presenting the events of a single summer's night, is but a prelude to a new and joyful life.

The economy of detail and the brevity of the poem are a means of conveying the impression made upon the lovers of the rapid passage of the summer night, which they perceived through a few highlighted details, and which turned to morning before they knew it.

Few Russian poets have equalled Fet's mastery in the writing of short lyrics. He made a notable contribution to this genre, a favorite with Russian poets of the 1820's and 1830's. He wrote: "In my work on verse . . . the main thing is not to exceed three quatrains; four is usually too many, for I am convinced that if I fail to strike the desired string I must wait for another moment of inspiration."[24]

After the changes wrought in the Pushkinian tradition of the lyric by Lermontov and Tyutchev, Fet introduced still further innovations. In order to understand them, let us analyze one of his most characteristic lyrics, "Distance." The poet's ability to pack meaning into every word is seen even in his choice of a title, the full significance of which becomes clear only on reading the entire poem. Even at first glance, the title suggests the poet's complex conception, since the word "distance" means at least two things: the measurable space between one object and another, and a point far removed, as "in the distance." In its essence, this poem, like the brief lyrics of Goethe, Pushkin, Lermontov and Tyutchev, is about man and nature. The original treatment of the theme in "Distance" justified a title that the ordinary reader, with his preconceptions of what a lyric ought to be, found unexpected:

> There   in   the   distance—
> Little   puffs   of   dust;

> Hoofbeats or footsteps?
> I cannot yet see.
>
> Ah, 'tis a rider
> On a galloping steed!
> My friend, dear and distant,
> Do not forget me!

This is more a film strip than a picture. If in "Whispers" the poet presented the flow of time, here he presents the flow of space through the observation of swift movement. The line "On a galloping steed" only confirms the impression the reader has already formed of the person's swift approach. The rhythm of the verse is that of hoofbeats. Only the second and fourth, sixth and eighth lines rhyme, so that the poem might have been arranged in four long lines, each interrupted by a caesura. But the poet needed the clipped rhythm of broken lines.

The first and second lines form a single sentence describing clouds of dust rising in the distance.

The third and fourth lines indicate that something is moving that the observer is as yet unable to identify.

In the fifth and sixth lines he sees that it is a horseman. At the end of the sixth, there is a sudden halt in the hoofbeat rhythm; there is a pause, a deliberate break, as the speaker, who until then has been merely an observer, suddenly is caught up by painful memories. The gay mood turns melancholy; the hoofbeat rhythm changes to a pensive one. The "lacuna" is so deep that there seems to be no connection at all between the first six lines and the last two. But the connection exists, and the reader divines it. The long pause invites a train of thought similar to the one that Pushkin develops in:

> Whoever has lived in dreary solitude
> Must know, and all too well, my friend,
> How oft a sleighbell's cheery chiming
> Doth raise a tumult in the heart.
> Perhaps it is a friend belated,
> A classmate of one's distant youth.
>
> And if it's she?—Oh heaven!
> Closer . . . closer . . . the heart must burst!
> But no, the sound is passing, is receding,
> Is dying—has died beyond the hill.[25]

Pushkin's poem, with a man speaking in the first person, offers only an approximate analogy to Fet's, in which the speaker is a woman. But undoubtedly the transition in thought implied by the pause is the one we have mentioned, and the reader finds it clearly expressed.

The writer Vladimir Korolenko, one of Fet's younger contemporaries, missed the implication that the speaker is a woman, but he gave the following interpretation, suggested by the pause: "Fet is undoubtedly a great artist. He enables us to feel the excitement of . . . the highway with clouds of dust rising above it; a guest is coming to the manor house!—perhaps the owner's beloved, bringing untold joy with her."[26]

Fet's innovation was the introduction of meaningful pauses into brief lyrics and the intensification of the implied rather than the direct message.

Only by deeply sensing the swiftness of the horseman's approach, and thereby estimating the dimensions of the distance out of which he comes; only by understanding the chain of associations arising in the poet's consciousness and evoking memories of a distant friend can we grasp the meaning of the poem and the full significance of its title.

There is reason to suppose that Fet's "Distance" was inspired by Goethe's "Nähe des Geliebten," the second stanza of which begins: "Ich sehe dich, wenn auf dem fernen Wege / Der Staub sich hebt." Goethe's poem, like Fet's, is about a woman's longing for her beloved. Both pieces are a woman's monologue, but they differ greatly in form. Goethe introduces one image after another; every couplet of his four-stanza poem offers a new scene. The poetic conception of the poem consists in the contrast between this ever-changing picture of nature and the constancy of the woman ever thinking of, ever waiting for, the man she loves. Fet, however, finds one picture sufficient, although this one picture is a dynamic, changing one. The poetic implications of the last two lines of Fet's poem enable the reader to feel the weariness of the woman's waiting as she stands gazing into the distance, and to share the wide range of sensations she experiences in a fleeting moment.[27]

The woman's anxious watching for the approaching horseman

in "Distance" bore for Fet the same lyrical message he had found in Pushkin's "The Burning Letter":

The logical precision of his skillful description of the burning process, more effective than exclamatory writing could be, speaks of an excruciating concentration of attention. . . . With every new phase of the burning, one cannot believe further destruction of the priceless letter possible. The description is charged with the most intense feeling. It ends in a cry of reconciliation—again "emotion."[28]

Fet's "Distance" also ends in a cry—the cry of a woman racked with longing for her absent lover. The restrained feeling underlying his description of swift motion ends in an unexpected burst of undisguised feeling.

We have already remarked that the poet's attention was concentrated on the problem of man's confinement within the narrow sphere of space and time allotted him by nature. This problem, to which he devoted much thought, cost him intense suffering. In the collection of 1850, however, he saw man and nature in a harmonious relationship. His sense of being bound to the earth and even to a definite spot on the earth did not yet oppress him; in fact, it lent warmth to his feeling for the universe, reality and concreteness to his sense of oneness with nature.

> I well understand the babe's soft prattle,
> Which speaks of the soul's acceptance of life;
> Deep in the heart sounds the unceasing babble
> Of a fount that springs with unspeakable joy.
> And I say to that star now gleaming so brightly:
> It's long since I've noticed your light in this world,
> Yet I verily grasp all the deep intimations
> Flashed from the sky by your all-seeing eye.

The poet does not regard being bound to the earth as a tragic limitation cutting him off from Heaven (compare Tyutchev's words "I, lord of the earth, am bound to the earth"). Nor is the thought of the limited time allotted to the individual on earth associated with the thought of death's bringing individual existence to an end. Fet's acute sense of the significance of the moment and the "expansion" of the moment under pressure of extraordinary content lead him to a poetic conception of life's flowering as a wonder so rich in meaning that it transcends all concepts of time and space.

There are moments when the stars descend to earth and when flowers unfold that blossom only once in a hundred years. The force of the marvelous is sufficient to suspend the laws of mundane existence.

Such moments are not only the fruit of subjective sensations; they also exist in nature, and it is given to some, if not to all, to identify themselves with nature and to enjoy a season of blossoming along with nature.

> We are alone; the moon shines in the garden,
> Gleams on the pane. . . . Dimly burn our candles.
> Your scented, your resplendent hair
> Falls in rippling locks upon your shoulders.
>
> Why are we silent? Is it the magic spell
> Of this May night, so luminous, so quiet?
> Or yet the brilliant singing of the nightingale,
> Pouring out his passion to the rose?
>
> Or the twittering of birds awakened by the shaking
> Of their nests in the wind beyond the alder bushes?
> Or the slow, slow descent of the stars,
> Coming down to us, their jealous rays atremble?
>
> Upon the coils of a fantastic bough the firebird,
> Denizen of fairytales and gaudy fantasies,
> Swings above the enchanted stream,
> His body cased in flame, aglow with emerald light.
>
> The seashells' patterned convolutions flash
> In myriad hues against the golden starlight,
> And every little whirlpool flings to the moon
> A foam of pearls, a spray of diamonds.
>
> Marvelous insects crowd on every leaf;
> All things expand, bursting their fetters.
> Many the familiar dreams that are awakened,
> Many the beliefs close cherished in the heart.

> Too soon the rainbow hues that teased the eye
> With their false promise fade away.
> Another instant and the tale is told;
> Again the possible alone holds sway.
>
> We are alone; the moon shines in the garden,
> Gleams on the pane. Dimly burn our candles.
> Your scented, your resplendent hair
> Falls in rippling locks upon your shoulders. . . . (174–75)

Fet's contemporaries praised this poem highly, but as a mere fantasy. In the collection of 1856 it is even called "Fantasia." To make it more compact and severe in composition, the third quatrain was deleted:

> Does it mean that the flowers, most precious of gifts,
> Have opened their petals with wilful languor?
> That the cactus, hoary with centuries, has come
>   to a flowering
> And the banana, and the sacred lotus?

The omission of this stanza emphasizing the reality of the miracle taking place in nature did not alter the poem's general meaning, but it did add to its fantastic quality. The reference to the blossoming of rare flowers links this poem to Fet's later story "The Cactus," in which he makes a forthright declaration of the importance of unordinary moments in the life of nature, especially the moment of flowering.[29]

Faith in the eternal life of nature and in man's ability to merge harmoniously with nature pervades many of the poems of 1850. This philosophical approach confers upon them an air of peace and resignation.

CHAPTER 3

The St. Petersburg Literary Circle

I *The Problem of Anthological Poetry*

THE collection of 1850 was well received by the critics. Journals of such different trends as *The Contemporary, Notes of the Fatherland* and *The Muscovite* spoke of its high quality. Appreciation was likewise expressed by the periodical *Repertoire and Pantheon,* which began publishing his poems. Only *Library for Reading* remained faithful to its earlier disapproval of Fet's poetry.

But neither the fame it brought him, nor the recognition of his talent by fellow writers, nor the popularity of his poems, which spread to the most remote districts of the country, had any effect on the poet's circumstances. He continued to lead a dull existence as an army officer stationed in the provinces, pressed for money, and forced—or so it seemed to him—to renounce love for purely material considerations. In a letter to I. P. Borisov of December 30, 1850, he wrote that the only thing his life could be compared to was a mud puddle, and that his spiritual suffering was like the suffocation of a man buried alive.

He sought relief by applying for a transfer to the Guards. This he received and at the end of 1853 went to St. Petersburg, in whose suburbs the Uhlan regiment in which he was to serve was quartered.

On his way to St. Petersburg from the south he stopped off at the Shenshin estate of "Novosyolki," where he met Turgenev, a neighboring landlord. Turgenev immediately took a liking to him, though he disapproved of his respect "for systematized views of life,"[1] i.e., for philosophical systems. In 1854, in St. Petersburg, Fet made the acquaintance of Nekrasov, the most outstanding of the progressive poets and an editor of *The Con-*

70

temporary. This event led to his meeting other members of the editorial board and also contributors, including Ivan Panaev, Avdotya Panaeva, Alexander Druzhinin, Pavel Annenkov, Dmitry Grigorovich, and Ivan Goncharov. Nekrasov competed with Andrey Kraevsky, editor of *Notes of the Fatherland,* in trying to persuade Fet to contribute solely to his journal.

The deterioration of Russian relations with England and France impinged upon the poet's life by forcing him to leave St. Petersburg, where he had achieved a longed-for place for himself among writers, and accompany his regiment to guard the Baltic coast. The place he had won among the literary intelligentsia was secure, however; his St. Petersburg colleagues regarded him as a poet of great promise, who should be taking an active part in the literary life of the day.

Most of the writers grouped around *The Contemporary* were close to Belinsky: they had either formed their own views under his direct influence or had adopted his views and considered themselves his pupils. As became clear at the end of the 1850's and the beginning of the 1860's, people of different political and esthetic convictions held widely differing conceptions of Belinsky's teachings. Writers found it expedient to define their attitude toward Belinsky as the literature of the era developed. During the "grim seven years" of ruthless censorship and liberal disillusionment (1848–55), some writers came to a sharp break with Belinsky's ideas, especially those of his last period. The critic Druzhinin was one of them.

Although Belinsky was "banned" after his death in 1848 (any mention of his name was deleted by the censor), critics at the end of the 1840's and the beginning of the 1850's kept referring surreptitiously to his works. Belinsky's activities brought prose to the forefront in Russian literature and demolished the idols of Romantic poetry (among them the poet Benediktov, who had been worshipped during the 1830's). At the same time, Belinsky asserted the importance of poetry as the enunciator of ideals. He maintained that the moment had not yet come for prose to propound these ideals, since real life did not present appropriate material to the prose writer. Poetry, on the other hand, could meet this need if the individuality of the poet was equal to the task.

Belinsky considered Pushkin a poet of such stature. His appraisal of Pushkin coincided with Gogol's, who knew Pushkin personally and wrote of him: "The name of Pushkin suggests the idea of a Russian national poet. . . . Pushkin is an extraordinary manifestation, perhaps the only manifestation of the Russian spirit. He is what the Russian will develop into, what he will be in, say, two hundred years."[2] Contrasting, as did Gogol, Pushkin's short lyrics, "in which every word opens up endless vistas, every word is as illimitable as the poet himself,"[3] with the cascades of eloquence indulged in by the vulgar Romantics, Belinsky pointed out that Pushkin's lyrics in classical form revealed, through pictures of nature and concrete imagery, the ideal of the human spirit, strong and whole. In his article "Latin Elegies" Belinsky points to the great German poet Goethe and the great Russian poet Pushkin as mighty forces opposing the vulgarity of their surroundings and as spokesmen of the lofty, poetic ideal—poets who, because they were free in spirit and spontaneous in expression, were capable of absorbing the poetic experience of the ancient world.

The term "anthological" was commonly used in referring to poems employing Greek and Roman imagery (taken mostly from mythology) and classical verse forms. Belinsky, however, included many of Pushkin's lyrical miniatures in this category, even though they treated of matters and were wrought in forms highly contemporary, and in no way followed the canons of ancient literature.

Belinsky considered the distinguishing characteristics of "anthological" poems to be complete lucidity of thought, grace, and conciseness of form. It was the clarification of "inexpressible" feelings and elusive sensations and their incorporation in harmonious forms that constituted the beauty of anthological poems. Citing "Son" ("The Dream"), a poem by Apollon Maykov, Fet's contemporary, whom Belinsky introduced to the reader as "a little known but highly talented poet," Belinsky asserted that this "anthological poem proves better than any argument that poetry is the expression of the inexpressible, the revelation of the secret, the clear and precise idiom of emotions that remain mute and mystifying when undefined."[4]

In other words, Belinsky regarded anthological poems not

only as an antidote for the ultra-Romanticism of the 1830's, but also as a means of freeing poetry from subjectivism. He criticized Apollon Grigorev's poetry for being too subjective and personal. He also criticized the "lyrical monologues" of Nikolay Ogarev for the Hamlet-like frankness with which they exposed the poet's tortured soul.

These and similar views held by Belinsky exerted great influence on the attitude of poets of the 1840's and 1850's toward anthological poems. Nekrasov, whose own poetry had little in common with the classical genre, spoke of them with the highest admiration: "The most difficult poetry to write is that in which to all appearances there is no message, no idea: I am speaking of landscapes in verse, pictures drawn with two or three brush-strokes."[5] Obviously, he is referring to only an *apparent* absence of idea, its expression through graphic images, and not directly. Nekrasov wrote these lines about the poetry of Tyutchev, Russia's greatest philosophical poet.

It is characteristic of the period that Nekrasov should have given preference to anthological poems, in which ideas are expressed only indirectly, and that he should have proclaimed the writing of such poems an intricate task worthy of the efforts of a true artist. It was only after a thorough analysis of Tyutchev's classical lyrics that Nekrasov presented a brief and rather superficial review of his other works, "in which the idea is the dominant element." But Tyutchev was primarily a thinking poet, the spokesman for a period in Russian history when all the energies of the avant-garde were concentrated on finding a philosophical conception of existence, on working out a "basic idea."

A tendency toward objectivity, toward a broad and many-sided view of life in its concrete manifestations, a tendency away from the domination of prevailing philosophical systems—such a trend was typical of Turgenev, too, who later announced: "I myself am naturally a Realist and a son of my times—but antiquity and classical forms in art are the things I most love and admire."[6]

Not only Belinsky's avowed followers, like Turgenev and Nekrasov, but even those who at the beginning of the 1850's had parted company with him—for example, Druzhinin and

Grigorev—reached the same conclusion by different paths: that Pushkin, as an objective poet and heir to the classical ideal of the harmonious individual, was the model to be followed by contemporary poets.

Nekrasov's article "Russian Minor Poets," which appeared in *The Contemporary* in 1849 and was devoted to an analysis of the poems of Ogarev, Tyutchev, and a number of less important poets, was one of the first efforts of *The Contemporary* to revive interest in poetry. As time went on, this effort became more persistent and systematic, a development that largely explains the cordiality with which Fet was welcomed into the *Contemporary* circle. Fet's departure from St. Petersburg did not disrupt his connections with this circle. In April 1855, Fet received a letter from Turgenev proposing a new and revised edition of his poems. "Nekrasov, Panaev, Druzhinin, Annenkov, Goncharov—in a word, all of our friendly circle send you greetings. . . . We would ask you to prepare a new edition of your poems, which well deserve meticulous revision and handsome presentation. . . . Why do you write to me of Heine? You are superior to Heine because you are broader and freer than he."[7]

This letter and the proposal it contained showed in what esteem the staff of *The Contemporary* held Fet, and also exactly what they most valued in him. By contrasting him to Heine, with whom Fet's friend Apollon Grigorev had compared him a little earlier (both of them, in Grigorev's opinion, represented "morbid poetry"), Turgenev indicated that he admired in Fet his "objectivity," the breadth and freedom of his world view, his independence from theory and lack of personal prejudices—qualities he did not find in Heine.

At the same time, Turgenev let Fet know that he found much that was not only undesirable but even unacceptable in his poetry. He warned him that preparation of the new edition required careful revision and strict selection.

II *Preparation of the 1856 Collection*

Fet expressed his willingness to ready the new edition and began intense work on it. In his copy of the 1850 collection

Turgenev marked poems, stanzas, and phrases with which he found fault. In the margin of this same copy Fet offered new versions, some of which were accepted, and others rejected.[8] Turgenev couched his disapproval and suggestions in sharp, peremptory form.

In later years Fet spoke with bitterness of his enforced subservience during the preparation of the 1856 collection.

Naturally I was profuse in my expressions of gratitude to the circle, and in the hands of its chief, Turgenev, work progressed rapidly. Almost every week I received letters with underscored verses and the demand that they be changed; I jealously defended my own version but, as the saying goes, "One man in the field is no warrior," and I had to submit to the majority opinion, as a result of which the collection edited by Turgenev came out more distorted than distilled.[9]

Many students of Fet's poetry consider the changes demanded by Turgenev a violation of Fet's rights as an artist and a mutilation of his work.[10] Boris Bukhshtab, however, to whose able scholarship we are indebted for the last two complete collections of Fet's poetry (1937 and 1959), rightly draws our attention to the fact that in later editions of his works Fét let stand the changes introduced in the 1856 edition. The work of the editor's hand comprised nothing but deletions. Turgenev did not add or change a single word. The poet himself made all the changes, after long and painstaking effort. Therefore, these revisions are not to be condemned lightly.

A close study of the 1856 collection led Bukhshtab to the conclusion that he must examine each change separately before deciding whether it improved or damaged the original version. He further observed that Turgenev's main purpose as editor was to remove all "muddy spots" from Fet's text—all that he and other members of the circle found "obscure."[11]

Some of the poems, which by that time had won wide recognition, became the subject of hair-splitting criticism by the members of the circle. For example, the phrase "the coils of a fantastic bough" from the poem "Fantasia" was the subject of extensive correspondence. Several versions submitted by Fet in response to his editor's demands were rejected. In the end, Turgenev wrote Fet a letter of "amnesty": "Don't torture yourself any more about the coils of that fantastic bough. Druzhinin has convinced us that the firebird, being a rococo creature, can perch only on a coiled bough, be it in a fresco or in a poem. And so we have agreed that this is not to be touched."[12] Behind his jocular reference to the firebird as a rococo creature, we sense Turgenev's annoyance with these discussions of "preposterous" epithets, unacceptable to a critic of the rational school—discussions in which he was forced to give way to Fet, who was supported by Druzhinin.

Turgenev's editing reduced the subjectivity of Fet's poetry by eliminating what he considered arbitrary associations and illogicalities. Actually it meant a changing of its basic tendency so that the objective, classical element became dominant. His resolute and logical pursuit of his aims led Turgenev into many a pitfall, especially when he came into direct conflict with the poet on the battlefield of his verse. A striking example of this predicament is his editing of the famous poem, "I Come to You with a Greeting." He struck out the stanzas about love and the creative impulse, attempting to turn the poem into a classical lyric by depriving it of the movement involved in the hero's recognition of the process taking place within him, and thereby transforming it into a static description of nature. Turgenev was particularly irritated by the poem's ending, which at that time he accepted as a statement about the unconscious, intuitive nature of art. Turgenev's revision did not make a classical lyric out of the poem. Instead of a harmonious whole, it became a damaged fragment.

Similarly, Turgenev did battle with Fet's unconventional philosophical views as reflected in his lyrics. Turgenev, who had received a serious philosophical education at the hands of German professors, looked upon Fet's ventures as feeble inanities which he dubbed "philosophoonings." Accordingly, he changed certain titles, among them "Distance." By removing this declarative title, Turgenev reduced the poem to a lyrical landscape without implied meaning.

The revision of certain poems and the deletion of others changed the entire character of the cycles and, consequently, of the book itself. The poem that introduced the collection of

1850 ("I Am a Russian, and I Love . . .") was completely redone. The beginning was deleted; the night scene was changed to a day scene which did not correspond with the ending of the poem; the series of images (including that of the lifeless, snow-covered plains), symbolizing the triumph of death, was disrupted. The poem lost its unity and key significance in the collection. Indeed, the "Snow" cycle could no longer be considered basic to the entire collection. It was transferred to the middle of the book from the beginning. With ruthless pen Turgenev struck out the fourth poem of this cycle: "Veter zloi, vetr krutoi . . ." ("A Bad Wind, a Mad Wind . . ."). In addition to the "Snow" cycle, the cycles "Fortune-telling," "Ballads," "To Ophelia," and "Melancholy" were reduced. The themes that suffered most from this editing were those of Russia and the inner conflict experienced by Fet's contemporaries. Many "Melodies" were also discarded.

It should be noted that in cutting the "Melodies" cycle Turgenev strove to retain only those poems dominated by pure sound and melody. He preserved all the ones in which music, sound, and song were the poetic theme. He rejected "Vesennee nebo gliaditsia" ("The Spring Sky Spreads Above Us") because he believed that the picture it painted of an evening on the Main River in Germany and the description of the poet's nostalgia distracted the mind from the sheer music of the verse and the emotions it evoked. Perhaps, too, the editor found this poem, the implied theme of which is also "I am a Russian" (it deals with the performance of Russian music in Germany), too subjective, too intimately connected with the poet's personal experience and therefore less comprehensible to the reader:

> Heavy is my heart with the secret
> Communed by the dying violins.
>
> 'Mid the noise of this alien crowd
> Their message is doubly clear.
> With magic power they remind me
> Of all that I hold most dear.
>
> Awakened memory summons
> The joys and griefs of the past,

And my heart contracts or rejoices
With every new run, every chord.   (176)

In other words, Turgenev introduced logic and singleness of
meaning into the structure of this cycle, which, by its very
name of "Melodies," should have expressed Fet's characteristic
principle of the subconscious, supra-logical nature of poetry,
a principle that was gradually to become his *profession de foi*.
He rejected Fet's intimations in this cycle of the close affinity
of sound and color. It is true, of course, that in the greatly
shortened poem "Ulybka tomitel'noi skuki" ("A Smile of Weary
Boredom"), the lines asserting that music "With languor and
sad insouciance / Transports us to its colorful world" are preserved, and in the poem "Fantasia" the adjective "brilliant"
is retained to describe the nightingale's song, but all other
poems in which brilliance and colorfulness are presented as
the main attributes of melody were stricken: "Pearls of the
orient—her teeth" (poem one); "As her sense becomes her, so
her sensibility" (poem two); "The morning mist rises from
the meadows" (poem four); "Has it been long since to those
magic strains . . . ?" (poem three); "When I do kiss your glisten-
ing locks" (poem ten); "With a tambourine in my hands and
delight in my eyes . . ." (poem eleven); "I will recognize at
once your snow-white veil" (poem twelve).

As a result, "Melodies" became a cycle of love songs and
poems about music. From the third place this cycle occupied
in the collection of 1850, it was moved to seventh. It is not
surprising that some students of Fet's poetry assert that Turgenev
proved in many instances to be indifferent to the melodic aspect
of Fet's verse. And yet our critical approach to Turgenev's
editorial efforts must not blind us to the beneficial influence he
exerted upon his "protégé" of those early years.

Without Turgenev, on whose initiative the collection of 1856
was undertaken and whose labor and enthusiasm carried it
through, the book might never have appeared; in addition, the
sympathy and support of *The Contemporary*, whose editors
and contributors were the foremost writers of the day, encouraged the young poet, stimulated his creative efforts, and
helped him endure the army service that left him little leisure

for writing. It is a common mistake to look upon the stern criticism of the composition, coherence, and artistic perfection of Fet's poetry by his new-found literary friends, men of high culture and refined taste, as a violation of his creative individuality, detrimental to the further development of his talent. The fact is that their judgment often aided the poet in perfecting his style and discovering for himself its distinguishing characteristics. The judges consulted by Turgenev were the most outstanding men of letters of that day, representatives of Fet's own generation and of his own artistic convictions, nor did they ever offer their opinions as final and infallible. Many of them continued to be enthusiastic admirers of Fet's poetry and maintained their professional ties with him for many years (Turgenev, Annenkov, Leo Tolstoy, and Vasily Botkin). It was Fet's desire not only to be understandable to his readers, but to be understood by them. What better readers could he have had for the purpose of verifying his poetic idiom than the men of letters gathered around *The Contemporary*? Pushkin's implacable demands of succinctness, precision, and effectiveness of artistic means, which these writers applied to Fet's spontaneous and impressionistic creations, put him through a severe school for developing his own critical judgment.

Following the traditions of the 1820's and 1830's, Fet sought to give each of his poems an effective ending, an unexpected turn revealing its meaning. Turgenev was opposed to these endings. We have already noted that in certain instances the deletion of the ending meant that editor and author differed basically over the very idea contained in the closing lines. In such cases, Turgenev's editing distorted the poem. But at other times, Fet's endings were added merely in accordance with prevailing tradition. An example of such conformity is "Spi— eshcho zarioiu" ("Sleep; As Yet the Dawn..."), which concludes with the banal coda:

> Soon a blush will liven
> Clouds and mountain tops,
> And the pallid features
> Of the sleeping streams. (695)

Turgenev struck this ending. Fet proposed another, but the editor, preferring that the poem should have no conclusion at all, rejected that too. He raised a similar objection to the quatrain ending the poem "Letnii vecher tikh i iasen" ("Still and Clear the Summer Evening"), a miniature depicting a village scene and ending:

> Do not, do not close the window!
> Linger here a little longer.
> What has happened? Why this longing
> To escape, to fly away?   (696)

Boris Bukhshtab has cited this editorial deletion as an example of the general trend of Turgenev's editing, which was to eliminate the subjective element in Fet's lyrics. Bukhshtab classified this poem as among those in which an ending is used for the sole purpose of shifting emphasis from the outer to the inner world, the world of the poet's emotional experience.[13] However, in this particular instance the "coda" is more objective than subjective. It withdraws us from the poetic mood evoked in the reader by the preceding lines and, by presenting a scene between two individuals—the poet and his prosaic companion who wishes to close the window—constitutes a plea for a lyrical response to the beauty of the evening. The reality of the picture reminds us of the scene from Tolstoy's *War and Peace* in which the romantic Natasha is unable to tear herself away from a contemplation of the night, while the prosaic Sonya is overcome by sleep.

In eliminating these and similar endings, Turgenev demonstrated that the meaning implied in the poems is clear without the addition of any logical conclusions. He showed that the reader himself will never close the window on the brief glimpse of eternal beauty revealed by the poet. Accordingly, the poem appeared in the following version:

> Still and clear the summer evening,
> See how drowsy droop the willows;
> In the west the sky is blushing,
> Silver-bright the winding river;

On the lofty wooded heights
The wind steals soft from crest to crest.
Hear that neighing in the valley?
There the horses are at play. (210)

III *Arrangement of the Collection of 1856*

Even in its external appearance the collection of 1856 was
a great improvement over that of 1850. The earlier book was
carelessly designed, printed on poor paper, and marred by
numerous typographical errors. The poems were set one after
another, so that a new one often began at the very bottom of
a page. The 1856 collection was designed with noble simplicity
and taste; each poem began on a new page; the text was carefully proofread; the book design reflected the classical spirit.
It opened with the "Elegies," that is, with a collection of verse
belonging to the genre that reached the height of its popularity
in the Pushkin period.

The arrangement of the cycles according to the principle
of contrast, adhered to in the 1850 edition, was retained in
that of 1856. The "Elegies," with their poetic restraint, were
succeeded by "In Imitation of Oriental Poetry," whose colorful
exoticism was tempered by the following poem, "To Ophelia."
The "Ballads" were placed adjacent to "Anthological Verse."
It should be noted, however, that in this edition there was a
marked weakening of the principle of contrast, a consequence
not so much of the rearrangement of the cycles as of the
alteration in their character resulting from the deletion of poems
that most vividly reflected the poet's characteristic way of seeing
the world about him.

The editorial distortion of the poem that introduced the
1850 collection, and the omission of the poem that expressed
its essence: "I Am a Russian, and I Love . . . ," as well as the
deletion of other verse belonging to the "Snow" cycle, funda-
mentally changed its significance. Alterations in the text of
certain poems from "Fortune-telling" deprived this cycle of
some of its "mystery." The "Ballads" suffered serious losses.
Two folk ballads, "Zmei" ("The Serpent") and "Metel'" ("The
Blizzard"), were omitted. The first told the tale of a black-
haired widow who "combed her tresses and bathed her neck"

in anticipation of the coming of her lover, the fire-serpent, who breathed flame above the thatched roof of her dwelling every night. The second was a drama of peasant life. A translation of Adam Mickiewicz's ballad, "Dozor" ("The Watch"), a poem about the ancient Slavs, was also omitted, as were the Romantic ballads "Sil'fy" ("The Sylphs") and "Geroi i Leandr" ("Hero and Leander"). The title of a ballad concerning a maiden languishing for her dead lover, who appeared to her while remaining invisible to others, was changed from "The Vampire," which cast the shadow of grim superstition upon the events recounted, to the dispassionate title of "Taina" ("The Secret"). "Poems for Children" then came to dominate the cycle, and the ballads were furnished the rational justification of being verse recited to the author by his nurse in childhood.

A certain rationalism, harmonious equanimity, and poetic restraint were characteristic of most of the poems comprising the "Elegies." As the first cycle in the collection, they did not have the thematic significance of the "Snow" cycle of the 1850 edition, nor even that of the "Fortune-telling" cycle. They did, however, foster the image of Fet as an "objective" poet. Among them were elegies reminiscent of the later Goethe's, and elegies of lyrical resignation as finely wrought as anthological verse. There were also gloomy elegies. The great variety of subjects treated and the wide range of qualities displayed by the persona and his beloved create the impression that the poet is a demiurge playing with the world, giving vent to any feeling that possesses him at the moment, refracting whatever comes his way through the prism of pure art, and dedicating himself to no one subject to the exclusion of all else. This trait of the "Elegies" did not, however, prevent the poet from formulating in them sharp moral and psychological conflicts and from offering his reflections on the philosophical problems that constantly absorbed his interest.

A mood of deep and bitter melancholy pervades the first elegy, addressed to a woman whose prosaic mediocrity the poet accepts intellectually but rejects emotionally. He is baffled by her indifference and cold courtesy; in his dreams, he confers upon her the richness of his own personality. He is ashamed of his own weakness and laments his fate:

> Alone, observed by none, my breathing labored,
> My face dark-burning with vexation and with shame,
> I frantically and futilely explore my mind
> To find an enigmatic aspect of the things you say;
> And mutter to myself additions and corrections
> Of words I so resentfully addressed to you,
> And in delirium, defying sense and reason,
> Shatter the darkness by calling out your name. (81)

In certain of his elegies Fet chose not to follow the traditions originating in the Weimar classicism of Goethe, nor yet those of the Russian Romantic school of the 1820's, but to adopt the psychological realism of Pushkin's last ten years. Fet's elegies revive the lyrical motifs of Pushkin's celebrated "Vospominaniia" ("Recollections"), so highly praised by Leo Tolstoy. Pushkin's poem reads as follows:

> At night, when all activity has ceased,
>   More lively writhe the snakes of conscience;
> Dreams do crowd, and the dejected mind
>   Teems with discontented thoughts.
> Before the inner eye memories silently
>   Unwind their endless scroll,
> And as I read the loathèd record of my days
>   I shudder and I curse,
> And bitterly complain, and weep as bitterly,
>   But nothing can erase the sad account.[14]

The qualms of conscience suffered by Fet during sleepless nights are always associated with remembrances of the love he betrayed. His recollection of first love invariably brings regret for his lost spontaneity and integrity of feeling, for everything connected with his better self, for being doomed ceaselessly to search for a moral haven where his soul can find peace.

> When in my dreams I'm ferried back to distant shores
> And find you rising out of veils of mist,
> Then do I weep with joy, like those sons of Judah
> Who first set foot upon the promised land. (81)

In the elegy "Ne spitsia" ("I Cannot Sleep"), the poet says
to the girl he had loved in days gone by:

> Why? What have I done? How am I guilty in your sight?
> And do my very thoughts of you deserve rebuke,
> That now your ghost should jeer so spitefully
> And fix me with incriminating eye? (87)

This deeply personal and tragic poem, in which the poet
generalizes a bitter life experience, appears among poems of
an entirely different order—poems about happy youth, and
requited love, and the joy of living, all presented in pensive,
elegiac form.

The poem "Postoi! Zdes' khorosho!" ("Stay! How Fair This
Spot!") was radically revised by the author for the collection
of 1856. The poem's main interest lies in its subject, which
is in praise of enclosed, sheltered space. Only in the silence
and solitude of limited space does the poet feel at home. The
proximity of the chaotic sea frightens him:

> Stay! How fair this spot! The shadow of the pines
> Lies in a wide dentate border etched in moonlight. . . . .
> How still it is! Yonder mountains make a wall
> Cutting us off from sounds of tumult and rebellion.
> No wish have I to go beyond the wall, where rocks,
> Cunningly escaping from beneath the heel of sheerest cliffs
> Tumble to the spiney shore where towering waves
> Rush up, rush back to the embrace of other waves. (82–83)

This might have been written in answer to Lermontov's
well-known poem "The Sail," in which a white sail is likened
to a strong and turbulent spirit cleaving the world as the
ship cleaves the sea and finding happiness only in storm
and struggle.

This same fear of the sea, which Fet perceived as a boundless, threatening element, and this same symbol of the sail,
now seen as a doomed creature afloat on the vast main of the
soul, is found in the poem "Staryi park" ("The Ancient Park").

The melancholy tone of the verse is set in the very first
stanza, describing autumn as a time of dying. Life's retreat

in autumn brings an end to life's joys, an end, in fact, to the world:

> Ready, resigned, the year's expiring blooms
> Are mournfully awaiting autumn's blast;
> The maple leaves are flaming at the edges,
> The dahlia drops her head, the rose her petals.
>
> Dawn spreads her glow above the somber forest,
> But now her brightness does not cheer the birds. (265)

Autumn brings an end to the world. (This ancient park once belonged to human beings, to a family; the sphere that was once theirs is disintegrating.) Fet always looked upon the grounds surrounding a house as nature, the "private" piece of nature belonging to man. In losing its owner, the ancient park lost its soul and its security, its defense against encroaching chaos.

> High upon a cliff a summerhouse is seen.
> I enter. Two lions, pawless, greet me on the stairs,
> And on the balustrade two names, unknown,
> Entwined, are half erased by time.
>
> I glance below. The tips of the unmoving pines
> Veer down in green and bristling wall
> To where a mountain path, carved by freshets,
> Twists like a yellow snake along the valley's bed. (265–66)

The poet is haunted by thoughts of the people who once enjoyed this cultivated spot, and his mournful impressions are crowned by a glimpse of the threatening sea on the horizon, which swallows up an unknown sail in the misty distance:

> I am alone. No step is following mine.
> My soul is desolate, intent my gaze;
> Beyond the pines stretches the sea,
> Unfeeling, uncompassionate, curving in a vast blue dome,
>
> A sail upon its crest white-gleaming like a gull.
> I wait to see it sink; it does not sink
> But, gliding slowly down the curved horizon,
> Vanishes in haze as cloud wisps melt in sky. (266)

The first cycle in the book, unified by the genre of the poems, had psychological and philosophical ties with the other cycles, especially with the nature and anthological lyrics. "In Imitation of Oriental Poetry" and "To Ophelia," which followed the "Elegies," were greatly reduced. Turgenev's editing, either by chance or with the intention of achieving a unity quite different from the unity Fet saw in the cycle, resulted in the retention of only two poems in the oriental section, both of them depicting passionate and impulsive love and the oriental ideal of womanhood. Among the verses omitted were some devoted to the language of flowers, and also several philosophical quatrains from Saadi. Editorial omissions and revisions of the "To Ophelia" series were aimed at removing all discord and contradictions from Fet's conception of Ophelia and at eliminating the cynical irony and subjective appraisal from Hamlet's attitude toward her. In the new version, Ophelia becomes a harmonious ideal, the incarnation of pure faith, a bright harbor in which the poet's soul takes refuge—and nothing more. Gone are the vagaries of the contemporary woman's character. She is elevated to an ideal to be worshiped instead of the flesh-and-blood woman the persona of the poems loved and tortured. This new Ophelia stood as the sublime, Northern ideal of womanhood as contrasted with the earthy, oriental concept. As this contrast developed, the image of Hamlet, the hero of the cycle, was simplified out of existence. Stripped of his subjective views and resentful irony, he was transformed into a melancholy symbol worshiping a fleshless ideal of beauty.

The anthological poems became the heart of the book, not so much because of their content as because of their classical style, which determined the character of the collection as a whole. Their influence is felt in the "Elegies," in "Evenings and Nights," and in "Miscellany."

IV   *The Anthological Poems*

The poem of this cycle that enjoyed the greatest success was "Diana." In the margin of his copy, so generously sprinkled with critical and sarcastic remarks, Turgenev wrote beside "Diana": "This is a *chef d'oeuvre.*" The poem's praises were sung most frequently in the middle of the 1850's and the beginning of the 1860's. Nekrasov said of it that "no praise is too high for this lofty poetry, which is as a refreshing draught to the soul." Nekrasov further noted the poem's wholesome moral influence, suggesting its superiority to the morbid poetry of the day.[15] Vasily Botkin, also an ardent admirer of "Diana," was most struck by the poet's extraordinary portrayal of the esthetic perception of a work of plastic art. "Fet's 'Diana' is a perfect jewel of anthological poetry," Botkin wrote. "Never before has the mute poetry of sculpture been felt and expressed with such force. These lines have truly imbued the marble with mysterious life."[16]

Fyodor Dostoevsky did not view the poem as a model of detached esthetic contemplation, nor as an exposition of an esthetic principle. "The last two lines of the poem," he asserted, "are so pregnant with impassioned vitality, yearning and significance that the whole of Russian poetry can offer nothing to compare with them in force and vitality."[17]

This short poem about a statue of the virgin goddess Diana, held by some ancient cults to be the patron of women during childbirth, appears to be merely descriptive. In reality, it contains within itself reflections on the nature of art and its relation to life. Wherein lies the force of a work of art? What does a poet see in it?

> I glimpsed the lovely contours of the maiden goddess
> Between the trees, poised above clear waters,
> In all the glory of her glistening nudity,
> Her wide eyes long and colorless,
> Her body motionless, in rapt attention.
> To the supplications of her sisters in the throes
> Of childbirth the marble maid was listening.
> Suddenly a morning breeze came through the trees,
> And on the waters her reflection stirred;
> I thought she now, with bow and quiver,
> Would whitely streak away among the trees,
> Off to her native Rome, city of eternal glory,
> To gaze again on Tiber's yellow flood,
> On clustered columns. . . . But no, the marble glistened
> Motionless in dawnlight with beauty incomprehensible.   (227)

Everything would seem to make this poem a model of anthological poetry: its classical atmosphere, the admiration it expresses for plastic beauty, its reflective mood, its harmonious
style, in which all its constituent parts, from general composition down to each separate word, are precise, polished, elegant.
Yet there is an element in the poem which sets it apart from
the ordinary monothematic anthological poem. The element
expressing this antianthological tendency within an anthological
poem is contained in the generalization of the last two lines
(those noted by Dostoevsky) suggesting the mystery, the in-
explicability of art. Such an ending was an innovation in
anthological verse, as was the lyrical feeling pervading it: on
the one hand, a sense of the fullness of life; on the other, a
yearning to discover the answer to art's mystery.

From the very beginning, the poet finds the statue ambivalent:
she lives and lives not, feels and feels not, moves and moves
not. Her eyes are colorless, she does not see, but her head is
raised high, which means she can raise her head, and it is
only her intense concentration that prevents her from moving.
She is listening to the groans of those suffering the pangs of
childbirth, but instantly the poet remembers that sympathy
is a feeling alien to her ("the marble maid"). A stirring of her
reflection caused by the wind on the water and it seems her
immobility is over; the moment has passed and will be succeeded by a burst of movement. The statue will acquire the
power of vision and will look once more on Rome, the yellow
waters of the Tiber, the clustered columns. Yet it is not this
animation of the inanimate marble that is presented as a miracle,
but the statue's continued immobility, the absence of the
expected, the sensed, the almost achieved animation. In this
portrayal of a poet's response to a work of plastic art, Fet
gives full expression to his esthetic tenets. He held that the
mystery of a work of art lay in its simultaneously belonging to
two spheres: the sphere of things lifeless, immobile, change-
less, and eternal; and the sphere of the constantly flowing, ever-
changing. Art frees life from its inevitable companion, death;
reveals the significance of the passing moment; recreates life
forms so complete, so mature, and so perfected, that they
tremble on the edge of change, of transition into other forms.

At the same time, art constrains life; it inhibits the unfolding of processes apparently ready to unfold. It confers immortality upon the passing moment.

The remaining anthological poems in this collection do not hold such philosophical meaning. But in his later lyrics Fet would employ philosophical themes combined with classical imagery and classical verse forms. The concept of the unity of opposites, such as eternity and the passing moment, life and death, beginning and end, was of central importance to him.

Fet's nature poetry was influenced by the anthological style and became imbued with the philosophical notion of the beginning as the source of all movement and the point at which the meaning of a process is concentrated. A poem that illustrates this idea is his "Pervaia borozda" ("First Furrow"), printed in *The Contemporary* in 1854 and included in the collection of 1856.

> Again the rusty plowshare flashes
> Where the bowing bullocks passed,
> And the new-cut furrow follows
> In a sable velvet band;
>
> Something fresh, something tender,
> Is diffused by vernal rays.
> In the footsteps of the plowman
> Come the rooks in ravenous tribe.
>
> Sweetly are the breezes laden
> With the scent of soil upturned—
> And young Gaea's bed is waiting
> To receive brave Jupiter.   (263)

Early spring, the first furrow, the first combining of the elements of light, sun and clear skies with the elements of the dark earth, full of mystery; this poem about beginnings sums up the story of nature in its entirety, for the beginning is the most meaningful moment of the whole process.

It is interesting to note that man, bullocks, and rooks are participants in this beginning, and it is they who form a nexus between heaven and earth. The efforts of each are equally important and significant. A belief in the affinity of man and beast and a sense of their equality in nature were, as we know, important elements of Fet's poetic credo. The lines "In the footsteps of the plowman / Come the rooks in ravenous tribe" sounded odd to many of Fet's contemporaries: they were parodied more than once. Aleksey Tolstoy, a poet and dramatist of that day, whose esthetic principles resembled Fet's in many respects, ended a satirical poem "Mudrost' zhizni" ("The Wisdom of Life") with these identical lines.

In the anthological poem "Zeus," written in 1859, Fet expressed his conviction of the importance of "beginnings" with particular clarity. He presents Zeus, lord of the universe, at his "beginning," in infancy, soon after his birth:

> In a Cretan cypress wood
> Rhea's infant son is crying,
> Angrily his little hands
> Seek and find his nurse's nipples.
>
> Full of hatred is the god,
> And his crying speaks of vengeance,
> Though as yet earth sees him not,
> Nor is he heard in heaven.   (300)

It would be difficult to state more explicitly that to the new, the weak, the unknown, the newborn, belongs the world. Zeus is not yet Zeus; no one has even heard his name; he is merely "Rhea's son." So far, the only thing he is lord over is the breast of his wet nurse. But his future begins with his infancy, and it is precisely at this time, when "earth sees him not / Nor is he heard in heaven," that he is most eminently a god, for in him at this moment are concentrated all the forces that are to determine his development and make him supreme over all.

V   New Lyrical Themes

As we have noted above, the theme of "beginnings" appeared in Fet's lyrics in the 1840's, bringing with it a joyous, affirmative attitude, a buoyant mood, sub-themes of love, spring, and creative activity. The poem "Eshcho vesna" ("It Still Is Spring"), first printed in the 1850 collection and greatly revised for that of 1856, is exceptional among his early works. Here the poet depicts spring as the birth of the new, at first weak and fragile, yet containing within it the guarantee of its future strength. Spring is the source of new love, new meetings, new ties. Fet begins the poem with:

> It still is spring—the garden seems possessed
> By a presence not of earth: some spirit of the night.
> I walk in silence, and slowly by my side
> My own dark shadow walks.... (134)

As the joy of spring is accompanied by the young poet's dark shadow, so the joy of beginnings is linked with grim thoughts of endings, and now the "diptych" becomes not birth and the life process culminating in a great flowering, but birth and death:

> Gloom has not yet settled on the tree-lined paths;
> The heavenly dome gleams blue between the boughs
> As on I walk. A fragrant coolness fans
> My cheeks. I walk. The nightingales are singing.
>
> Once more I contemplate the unattainable—
> The unattainable in this poor world of ours—
> And deeper, and more joyfully I breathe,
> And long to clasp—ah, someone to my breast!
>
> The time will come, and very soon perhaps,
> When, though the earth again be yearning for renewal,
> This heart will cease to beat for all eternity,
> Will cease to love, will cease to long for anything. (135)

In the collection of 1856 this connection of beginnings with endings occurs more often than in the lyrics of the 1840's.

The tragic conception of the end is intimated in "Vesna na dvore" ("Spring Has Come..."), describing the awakening of nature and the exultation it brings to man. This little masterpiece consists of six lines presenting a wonderfully fresh and concrete picture of spring, then two concluding lines shifting to a philosophical plane. Between the sixth and seventh lines is a transitional pause suggesting a chain of reflections on the immortality of nature, capable of endless renewal, and on the brevity of man's life, which knows no renewal. The juxtaposition of life and death is accompanied by a juxtaposition of man and nature. Owing to the extraordinary technical skill in writing miniatures which Fet developed in the 1840's, he was able to compress so rich a content into two quatrains!

> What fresh, invigorating air!
> No words can do it justice—none!
> How loud, at noontide, runnels in the gulley
> Spin their silvery skeins against the stones!
>
> Birdsong trembles in the ether, fades;
> Rye is greenly sprouting in the field—
> And soft a gentle voice is singing:
> "Another spring, and you alive to greet it!"   (137)

Fet expressed a similar idea by other means in a prose story and in the poem "Bol'noï" ("The Sick Man"), the latter depending for its effect largely on thoughts suggested rather than stated. Nature's renascence in spring causes a sick man to long for this season's return in the hope that it will bring him, too, new life. As he lies gazing out of the window he eagerly notes each sign of spring. But nature's revival has nothing to do with him. The harmony between man and nature has been destroyed, and man ends his life's cycle unaware of the estrangement.

Despite the external similarity between man longing for the return of spring and nature "yearning for renewal," the implication of the poem is that the lack of harmony between them will bring about the death of the sick man at the same time that nature is enjoying her rebirth.

In this poem Fet reveals what, for him, is a new sensation: horror of confinement, of limited space, a feeling conveying his subconscious sense of the great gulf dividing man from boundless, deathless nature:

> He stared about him as at prison walls,
> Then to the window turned his burning gaze,

And ah! how longed to be in open spaces!
How longed to breathe the air the birds were breathing!

Beyond the windowpane the days, like fragile dreams,
Came soaring out of rosy east on wider wings;
Despite the frosts that lingered on, the sun
Hung crystal drops along the rims of roofs.

One thought possessed him as the days went by:
"The skies of spring will surely bring me health." ·
He waited. Soon the smells of spring must burst the window,
And there—two swallows mating on a bough!   (260)

Here we find a tendency that became characteristic of Fet's
later lyrics. The poet does not proceed from an immediate
observation of spring to thoughts of life and death, but from
the imminence of death to a longing for life and identification
with deathless nature. He displays a new attitude toward birds,
too, treating them not as man's companions, inhabitants of
one and the same sphere, but as dwellers in an entirely different
world, the world of limitless space, as endless as the life of
nature and as inaccessible to man.

This new feeling of abhorrence roused in Fet by limited
space as contrasted with the boundless sky is expressed in
"Reval" (the pre-Revolutionary name of Tallinn), which, for
the 1856 edition, was given the subtitle "Lines Written on
Hearing 'Der Freischütz.' "

The theatre is dark and empty. Agatha
At last is safe within her lover's arms,
And I, still in the arms of music,
Wander light of heart through narrow streets.

Everything sleeps. Between the cliffs of houses
The sky is flowing like a spangled stream.
The clatter of cart and carriage wheels
At distant crossroads has subsided;

With every step the crowded city
Closes tighter, locking me in,
But there, on that high balcony,
A light is shining, a piano sounds. . . .

> In silvery cascades of melody,
> Along a beam cleaving the darkness,
> Your voice mounts freely to the stars,
> And in my heart its harmonies find echo.   (271)

It is of significance that this is an urban poem. In his cycle of urban poems entitled "Evenings and Nights" in every case the poet observed the city through the window:

> Somehow I breathe more easily at night,
> More deeply, somehow. . . .
> Even the city does not press upon me.   (207)

In "Reval," he not only finds himself walking in city streets, but streets in a medieval, Gothic city, which are so narrow they shut off the view of the horizon. In his copy of Fet's poems, Alexander Blok, the eminent twentieth-century Russian poet, underscored the lines "Between the cliffs of houses / The sky is flowing like a spangled stream." These lines do indeed convey strikingly a sense of urban confinement, which here symbolizes the limited and pressing span of human life. Art in general and music in particular free man from the consciousness of his spatial limitations by furnishing him with wings to bear him above the earth. The theme thus introduced in "Reval" was destined to be richly elaborated in Fet's verse of the 1860's and 1870's. Again and again in those years, he was to convey the impression made by music by comparing it to flight, to a lifting off from the earth and a commingling with the air.

So keen was Fet's sense of nature as a continuous process, as a perpetual flux and flow, that he was led not only to meditate upon and seek the deeper meaning of beginnings and endings and find in this search a source of themes and imagery for his lyrics, but he was also brought to look upon every passing moment chosen for portrayal as a moment of transition, one link in an endless chain of changes in man and nature. "Fet seeks to fix moments of alteration in nature. . . . Fet takes particular pleasure in describing brief moments of transition—boundary situations," Bukhshtab has written.[18]

This characteristic trait of his poetry, evident even in the 1840's, was further developed in the 1850's.

One might say the poet not only chose transitional moments and moods as a subject for portrayal, but also accepted the very fact of change and transition as an esthetic element, an element of the beautiful. But the reading public, even in the 1850's, found the portrayal of movement in nature too odd, too indefinite, too meager to serve as total subject matter.

In reference to Fet's poem "Zhdi iasnogo na zavtra dnia" ("Await Clear Skies Tomorrow"), one of his most delicate and inspired creations, in which the details selected build up to a picture outwardly still but inwardly full of imperceptible movement marking the change from day to night, the critic Boris Almazov, friend of Grigorev, wrote testily: "The vagueness of the poem could not be more complete." He follows up this statement with quotations, on which he comments contemptuously: "What sort of stuff is this?"[19]

Almazov considered a poem that merely describes the transition from day to night empty and meaningless.

"Await Clear Skies Tomorrow" belongs to a cycle called "More" ("Poems of the Sea"), begun when Fet's regiment was sent to Estonia to guard its Baltic seacoast in 1854 and 1855. The cycle was augmented by poems written during travels on the Black Sea and a vacation in Italy (1856–57). A few poems date from Fet's latter years. When toward the end of his life he prepared a complete edition of his works, he united all these poems in the cycle "Poems of the Sea," which is not to be found in the 1856 edition.

In "Await Clear Skies Tomorrow" Fet records a new impression received from, and a new attitude adopted toward, nature. The sea is no longer a hostile and dreaded element. The poet is separated from the limitless horizon by the ships "drowsing" in the harbor, but this limitation of space is relative. True, the ships' flags are but faintly stirring in a breeze that could not possibly fill their sails and bear them away, and yet these ships are not the primeval forest that shut out the horizon in the poems of the 1840's. In their very essence, ships are meant to slice through space and not block it off; it is only the time—the moment of transition from day to night—that transforms them temporarily into a barrier standing between the harbor and the boundless sea. This change is not enough to disturb the poet's composure.

Later, Fet explained that his chance to observe the sea constantly, day and night, had enabled him to develop a new lyrical feeling for it and to create for himself another, more real and exact image of it. Days spent on the seashore, nights sleeping in a summerhouse built directly over the sea, enabled him to make the intimate acquaintance of an element he had scarcely known before. "In the course of the summer I had an opportunity to observe the sea in all its many aspects," he recalled. He named its three primary moods as perfect calm, slight agitation, and storm, adding: "But how can one convey, how can one even hint at the subtle modulations from one state to another? Here is the beauty of the sea and a sea of beauty! My daily proximity made me its votary, as witness my poems of the sea, which at the time were received most sympathetically by Turgenev's literary circle."[20]

In the new cycle, Fet appears to have set himself the aim of showing the vast variety of the sea's moods, and in this movement and variety to reveal the beauty and richness of life. The poet observed the waters from the shore, but they drew him, even hypnotized him: "Whenever I pass that ancient willow / I must turn for a view of the bay" (241), he writes in the poem called "The Bay." In other poems of the same cycle, he stands on the shore facing the sea and is unable to take his eyes away from the endless diversity and movement of what at first glance seems a static body of water. He is fond of watching the approach of a single wave, which completes its life span by breaking on the beach, following the pattern of all the waves that have come before and will come after it.

This response to, and representation of, the sea record Fet's personal way of seeing things. Just as for him time is constructed of a series of moments varying in intensity according to content, and space is built up of limited circles, of the delineated "spheres" surrounding the individual, and the life process itself is a constant transition from one state to another, so then is the vast panorama of nature divided into separate objects and phenomena, each of them, even though it be the same as numerous others, having its own particular significance and its own fulfillment.

Fet's personal lyrical representation of the world must be considered in association with the analytical nature of Russian Realism of the middle of the nineteenth century. As the Soviet scholar Gromov has correctly observed, Fet's "lyrics of transitional states" derive from the tendency of psychological realism to dissect a single emotion, study it, then reproduce it from the elements of which it is composed.[21] Despite a new note of reconciliation with the watery element, all the sea lyrics of the 1850's and 1860's are characterized by the author's vital awareness of his attachment to, and his oneness with, the earth. His poem "Na korable" ("Sea Journey") again expresses his distrust of this perfidious and alien element. The poet's fear of chaos recurs with its former strength, and he feels with new intensity that he belongs to the limited, the dear and familiar earthly sphere that he trusts like a child:

> We fly! The earth skims past the ship
> In a vast and misty blur;
> Beneath the boards on which I stand
> An unfamiliar element
> Is heaving, spewing foam and spray;
>
> And heaves my heart, and dully aches.
> What matter that the sea's rim shimmers bright?
> My soul is captive in a foreign sphere
> To which a force mysterious
> Against my will conveyed it.
>
> I seem to have a foretaste of that day
> When I, without a ship, shall sail
> Upon the airy ocean, leaving behind
> Beloved earth to vanish in the mist. (243–44)

Finding himself in the power of the chaotic sea, the poet is unable to accept its changes as an expression of the fullness and richness of life. He finds it perilous, a dread and unfamiliar element signifying death.

VI *Lyrical Monologues*

Richard Gustafson devotes a whole chapter of his book on Fet to what he calls "the addressed monologue."[22] He classifies many of Fet's lyrics as such but explains that the addressee is an abstraction and the conversation is really an analysis of the persona's emotions spoken silently to himself.[23]

It is true that many of Fet's lyrics are cast in the form of spontaneous and impassioned communications of his feelings, declarations of his impressions in the process of recognizing and appraising them, and expressions of his thoughts in the process of conceiving and elaborating them. It is equally true that in many instances the strength of his emotions and impressions reduce to insignificance the woman (the "beloved") to whom they are addressed. But at least in his early lyrics this woman was not an abstraction or an object of indifference to him.

We have noted above that Hamlet, the spokesman of the cycle "To Ophelia," is a personality no more rich and complicated than Ophelia herself, to whom he pours out his heart. For that reason Ophelia may be placed on the same plane as the oriental women who speak in the first person in the cycle "In Imitation of Oriental Poetry." It was Fet's ability to conceive strong and striking women that enabled him to speak for them in so many of his poems, including those from the cycles "Fortune-telling," "Ballads," and "Miscellany." We hear the voices of vivacious girls in village huts; pensive noblewomen; sad women, abandoned by their husbands; passionate southern belles; stern, kind mothers; and superstitious nursemaids devoted to their charges. The characters of many of Fet's women are mysterious, complicated, exalted, doomed, and sometimes so elusive that the poet himself cannot grasp them. It is such women whom we meet in the monologues "Ia znaiu, gordaia, ti liubish' samov-last'" ("I Know, Proud Maid, You Love to Wield Your Power"), "Ia znal eio maliutkoiu kudriavoi" ("I Knew Her as a Curly-headed Child"), and "O, ne zovi! Strastei tvoikh tak zvonok rodnoi iazyk" ("Oh, Call Me Not! Our Native Tongue Rings With Your Passions").

Some of Fet's poems are "inner monologues," revealing, as

in confession, the innermost workings of a woman's soul and portraying the feminine character in relation to the circumstances and events which throw it into relief, for example "The Secret," "Sestra" ("Sister"), and others.

Poems addressed to Mariya Lazich and those presenting her image are imbued with a spirit of tragic fatality: "V dolgie nochi, kak vezhdy na son ne somknuty" ("In the Long Nights, My Eyes Unclosed"); "Neotrazimyi obraz" ("Compelling Image"); "Starye pis'ma" ("Old Letters"); "Alter Ego"; "Ty otstradala, ia eshcho stradaiu" ("Your Suffering Is Over, Mine Goes On"); "Dolgo snilis' mne vopli rydanii tvoikh" ("For Long I Heard Your Sobbing Cries"); and others. The story of this wrecked, early love that still holds Fet in thrall runs like a leitmotif through all his verse of the 1850's and 1860's; against this background there arises a new image, that of a young, impetuous and impassioned girl, incapable of understanding the poet's bitter experience. In her, the poet seeks a haven for his tortured soul. She brings comfort, faith and blithe innocence into his funereal world. This young creature is not the doomed, incorporeal Ophelia, nor is the hero the suffering egotist of Fet's first book of verse, only too willing, according to Apollon Grigorev, to find pleasure in indulging his grief.[24] The relationship of the hero to his new and youthful beloved is determined by the depth and reality of his suffering, his disappointment in the path he has taken in life, his disillusionment with wordly values, and a longing for life and happiness despite the bereavement he can never forget. He is tenderly solicitous of her untainted spirit, which lives by simple and eternal values. She brings him the happiness of human communication and transports him to a sphere "where storms pass us by, where impassioned thoughts are pure." Such a woman in Fet's favorite setting of the homecircle (comparable to Pushkin's ideal of "fireplace comfort") is presented with such charm in the following poem that, set to music by Pyotr Bulakhov, it soon became one of the most popular drawingroom songs in Russia:

> When the shadows of evening are falling
> I wait for the ring of the bell;
> Come to me, come, little darling,

We will sit by the fire, you and I;
I will snuff out the quivering candles—
Sufficient the light of the logs;
To your merry chat I will listen
To ease the ache of my heart;
To your childish dreams I will listen,
And pray that they be fulfilled;
At the sound of your voice my feelings
Well up till I press back the tears.
Before dawn we will rise and I gently
Will tie your scarf 'neath your chin,
And we'll walk over patterned moonlight
Till we come to your garden gate.

The poet's relations with this young lady are without bursts of passion and without the conflict resulting in mutual attraction and repulsion. He yearns to be in her presence and eagerly shares her inner world. It is she, this simple, innocent soul full of trust and given to happy daydreaming, who leads the conversation, while he, the intellectual who has thought and suffered so much, listens eagerly and in silence to her "chat," feeling that the choking pain within his breast is about to be relieved by a flow of healing tears.

Even in the 1840's self-contemplation became an essential and consciously induced stimulus to Fet's creative activity. His contemplation of the objective world and of himself as part of this world was the root from which his poetry sprang. This led Apollon Grigorev to liken Fet's artistic method to that of the "naturalistic school," which was part of the new Realistic trend in Russian literature of the 1840's.

Fet himself considered the ability to observe and reveal new qualities in nature and in human psychology the principal element of a writer's talent. The men of letters grouped about *The Contemporary* agreed with him in this and regarded him as a discriminating observer and an author who recorded his observations accurately and answered for their truthfulness. The poem "Na Dnepre v polovod'e" ("On the Dnieper in Spate") is dedicated to Avdotya Panaeva, Nekrasov's common-law wife and a member of the literary circle associated with *The Contemporary*. This poem is a living picture of nature; in it, at no point does the poet directly address his companion, and only at the very end does he openly reveal the idea glimpsed darkly in the picture. And yet this poem, too, is a monologue addressed to his companion—not, this time, the impulsive young creature who has captured his heart, but a woman his own age, with similar interests, tastes and, to a certain extent, life experience.

The lyrical content of this poem resembles that of many of Nekrasov's poems. It paints a picture of the "healing" expanses of nature in the depths of the poet's native land. Here the themes of Lermontov's "Native Land" are reduced to the single lyrical theme of contrast between the calm of wide open spaces and the spirit of revolt animating that "eternal wanderer," the Russian intellectual.

It is characteristic that Fet's wide open spaces are more "confined" than Lermontov's. Lermontov's Russia is the cold and silent steppe, the boundless, heaving forest, and rivers that resemble seas. Fet, on the other hand, sees the vastness of a single river, the Dnieper, in spate, and at that particular point at which their sailboat is crossing it. He sees it from shore to shore, noting the changes incidental to their crossing and thereby conveying a feeling of its wide expanse. He communicates a sense of the overpowering force of the elements by describing them in a state which, if not the usual, is nonetheless a characteristic one.

The first stanza, with enjambment severing the paradoxical metaphor and thereby stressing its originality, sharpens our senses for the reception of this unusual picture and causes us to make the special effort, necessitated by syntactical difficulties, of taking leave of the shore and plunging into the river's swift current:

It was growing light. The wind buckled the resilient glass
Of the Dnieper without a single sound arising from the waves.
The old riverman set out, pushing off with his pole,
Grumbling the while at his grandson. (258)

The ensuing lines describe the struggle with the river and the subtle shifts in the relationship between boat and water throughout the course of the journey. They also present

pictures revealed by an ever-changing point of view as the boat
gains speed:

> And there an inundated wood flew past . . .
> Mirror-like bays had pushed their way inside it;
> A greening poplar rose above the sleepy waters,
> And the white froth of apple trees, and quivering willows.
>
> (258)

In the first version of the poem published in *The Contemporary*, the poet's presentation of the vast panorama of the flooding
river was followed by a lyrical conclusion in which, awed by
the majesty of nature, he condemned the vanities of city life.
This ending, like many others, was deleted in the 1856 collection,
only one line of it being retained as fully expressing the thought
intimated by the descriptive text: "Here would I remain an age
to breathe, to gaze, to listen. . . ."

This poem made a deep impression on Turgenev, but
unquestionably he found the description of nature more significant and artistically important than the sententious conclusion.

CHAPTER 4

Afanasy Fet in the 1860's

I *Esthetic Disputes of the Late 1850's and Early 1860's*

FET'S collection of 1856 was a great and lasting success. "All our journals received Fet's book with praise and good will," wrote Vasily Botkin, noting, however, that the praise was limited to the literary élite and was incomprehensible to the average reader. "In a word, his success may be said to be only literary, and we attribute this to the very nature of his talent,"[1] the critic went on. Considering Botkin's immediate observation of the public's as well as the critics' response to the volume, it is difficult to suppose that he could have erred, and yet quite the opposite opinion was expressed a few years later by the prose writer Saltykov-Shchedrin:

A good half of his poems exude the most sincere freshness and al-most the whole of Russia is singing songs set to his words. . . . If, despite all this sincerity and all this lightness of touch that instantly captivates his readers' hearts, he must still content himself with the modest lot of a second-rate poet, the reason for this, it seems to us, lies in the narrowness, the monotony, the tightness of the world which Fet portrays in his poetry.[2]

We see, then, that in contrast to Botkin, Saltykov-Shchedrin bore witness to Fet's popularity with the general public, the ordinary reader, at the same time doubting that his works would stand the test of serious esthetic criticism and denying him the right to be included among the best writers of his day.

There was nothing exceptional in this clash of opinion. Such diametrically opposed positions were taken with respect to the work of many writers at the end of the 1850's and the beginning of the 1860's, among them the plays of Alexander Ostrovsky and the novels of Ivan Turgenev.

103

Critical dissension reflected the sharpness of the esthetic disputes raging at the time. Fet was a fully established member of the St. Petersburg literary coterie at a time when it was deeply agitated by various movements. It was a period of new trends in art, new theoretical conceptions, bitter conflicts between proponents of opposite schools, and of pusillanimous attempts to hold to the middle road.

The upheaval in literary circles was closely connected with historical events within the country. The end of the despotic reign of Nikolay I, the dissatisfaction with serfdom felt by all classes of society, beginning with the peasants and ending with liberal-minded members of the nobility and bourgeoisie, preparations for peasant reforms, the sudden growth in influence of the class of untitled intellectuals (the *raznochintsy*), the rapid development of the natural and social sciences—all these factors served to stimulate thought, intellectual discussion, and criticism of beliefs and convictions.

Esthetic theories were a part of the ideological sphere in which began heated arguments that then spread to every branch of intellectual pursuit and soon assumed a political character.

In the statements quoted above, we see the efforts of Botkin, on the one hand, and of Saltykov-Shchedrin, on the other, to confirm their ideas of the beautiful and draw the poet to their respective sides. Botkin saw Fet as a poet "for the few," one who would not join forces with the rising writers whose platform demanded that an author serve the people and consciously subordinate his interests to theirs. Saltykov-Shchedrin reminds this poet, whose verse was so widely popular, that true artistic achievement depends on the artist's treatment of social and political problems of importance in the development of his native land. Nikolay Chernyshevsky, in his brilliant dissertation of 1855 entitled *The Esthetic Relations of Art to Reality*, opposed the idealistic conception of art; and Nikolay Dobrolyubov, who became the leader of revolutionary democratic criticism in the late 1850's, caused a split in *The Contemporary*. At the beginning of the 1860's Druzhinin, Botkin, Annenkov, Turgenev, Leo Tolstoy, Grigorovich, and other liberal-minded writers from the nobility ceased contributing to the journal.

Gradually Fet was drawn into these discussions of esthetics. For a while, his lyrical verse appeared in *The Contemporary* along with radical articles by such men as Chernyshevsky and Dobrolyubov. Fet was rather more attracted than repelled by literary arguments. In his early youth he hád been the sort of student who sought ideological conflict instead of avoiding it. In 1856, during a vacation granted him for the purpose of taking a cure, he met Turgenev abroad and the two engaged in such violent discussions of matters esthetic and political that members of the family with whom Turgenev was staying feared they would injure each other.

Fet sought to discover his own answer to esthetic questions, to reach an independent decision on the place of the writer in society. In 1856, Nekrasov, too, published a collection of verse, an event he anticipated by sending Fet his poem "Poet and Citizen," containing the declaration: "Poet you may not be, citizen you must!"—words that instantly flew from one end of the country to the other. In this poem Nekrasov defined contemporary aims, basing his conclusions on an analysis of the experiences of contemporary poets who had lived through the period of crushing political reaction after 1848. The revival of Russian society and the renewed interest in political affairs after 1855 shocked many writers. In Nekrasov's critical article on Tyutchev's poetry, written in 1850, the author hinted at his concern for his own fate and that of his contemporaries, men relegated by political oppression to the position of "second-rate poets," men deprived of the opportunity freely and harmoniously to develop their talent.

In order to state his own views on the poet's calling, Fet chose means similar to those of Nekrasov. Fet's collection of verse, like Nekrasov's, appeared in 1856. He also wrote a critical essay on Tyutchev, which contained a declaration of his esthetic principles and which appeared in the journal *Russkoe slovo* (*Russian Word*) in February of 1859. In the second half of the 1850's he began writing poems "with a message," in which he expressed his opinion on the place of poetry among other human activities.

Fet's solutions of esthetic problems, however, were often directly opposed to Nekrasov's. In "Poet and Citizen," Nekrasov addresses his colleagues, asserting that the change in the political situation within the country demands that they devote themselves to social themes in their writings and that they repudiate "pure lyrics" for the sake of propagandizing ideas of social progress.

For Nekrasov, as for other radicals of the 1860's, the idea that a writer's creed should be based on an acknowledgment of his duty to serve the cause of the people was linked with a deep faith in historical progress and a belief in the effectiveness of political activities in advancing this progress. Fet, on the other hand, did not believe in progress. Although in no sense an admirer of the existing system, he felt that not only was a struggle against it useless, but that even criticism of it was equally hopeless.

For him, the purpose of poetry lay not in the solution of social problems, nor in the analysis of contemporary life, but in the creation and preservation, through a sensual and psychic perception of reality, of a special sphere in which life, purified of vanity, discord, and chance, became a source of delight and of the flowering of the individual.

In his practical and social activities man is guided by reason, but this does not enable him to escape evil, the struggle for existence, and bitter disillusionment. He is constantly conscious of his dependence upon circumstances and upon the limitations imposed upon him by his position in society as well as by the state of society at any given moment. This awareness, according to Fet, shackled and humiliated the individual and deprived him of freedom. There was, he believed, no escape, for the moment one frees oneself from one form of dependence one falls into another. Art is the only realm in which one can know absolute freedom. "Certainly nobody assumes that ... we alone remain unaware ... of those periodic incongruities that would fill the heart of any man with ... grief for his country. But such grief cannot possibly be a source of inspiration," he wrote at a later date.[3]

According to the democratic writers and readers of the 1860's, the poet could gain public trust only by expressing grief for his country. "The most damning accusation of our times," wrote Herzen, "is grief 'in general.'"[4] For Fet, this was an emotion inimical in its very essence to free, creative activity. In poetry he sought, according to his own declaration, "an escape from all the griefs of daily life, including civic grief." At the same time, he suffered so severely from the contradictions and wrongs of the society in which he lived that he said he was like one whose clothes have caught fire and who throws himself into the water to extinguish the flames—water, in this instance, being poetry. In Fet's mind this simile was full of deep and heart-rending meaning, for the death of Mariya Lazich was caused by her clothes catching fire. Art, according to Fet, frees humanity from the perpetual struggle for existence, from cruel and unreasonable circumstances and inevitable rapacity. It makes man noble, independent, and all-powerful. Beauty is the great healer.

Fet's views on art were akin to those of Kant and his followers in that he attributed extraordinary significance to creative activities, placing them above practical activities and a capacity for logical thinking.

At the same time, he followed in Gogol's steps by asserting that art is essentially affirmative, that beauty undergirds it, and that the principal emotion expressed by lyric poetry is a love of life and a love of nature springing from a recognition of its beauty. In his "Uchebnaia kniga slovesnosti" ("Textbook of Literature"), published posthumously in 1896, Gogol wrote:

Beauty is the wellspring of poetry. On beholding the beautiful, man is inspired to praise it, to compose a song to it, to sing. To praise it in words that will enable others to sense the beauty of the object of praise. A poet is he who is more capable than others of perceiving the beauty of creation.[5]

This attitude toward the source of lyricism, which, in Fet's case was combined with social pessimism and a lack of faith in the ethics of "practical" action undertaken by individuals, or by humanity as a whole, was at the root of his action in offering the timeless themes of his poetry in opposition to the socially pressing topics of his contemporaneous world.

Unlike the radical and liberal intellectuals of the 1860's, who categorically demanded that literature deal with political and social topics of contemporary importance, Fet would have none of this. He was so determined and consistent in this regard that, when speaking of his fierce love of life, he excluded from his conception of life all political and social phenomena as well as whatever pertained to the sphere of logical thinking. "All of life is dear to me," he wrote to Leo Tolstoy on May 16, 1863. "How wonderful it is—with its mosquitos, cuckoos, mushrooms, flowers! Sheer joy!...As for science...it is but the observation of life."[6] He went on to draw a contrast between the eternal and absolute beauty of nature and the instability of human relations with their inevitable conflicts which, even against people's will, split them into opposing camps.

Fet's conception of beauty as the fullness of life; his conviction that everything in nature is beautiful and capable of purifying man's soul; his love of living representations of living reality and his striving to preserve them in art—all these approaches were shared by other Realistic writers of the day. Turgenev and Tolstoy inveighed vehemently and persistently against those who propagated "democratic esthetics," seeing in them advocates of the didactic school. Nekrasov held other views, yet in a criticism of Ostrovsky's play *You Can't Live As You Like*, in which Nekrasov detected Slavophile tendencies, he urged the playwright to create more freely, to rid himself of tendentiousness as fatal to art. Neither Tolstoy nor Turgenev, to say nothing of Nekrasov, accepted Fet's favorite belief (reflecting Schelling's esthetics) that only in creative activity and esthetic perception may the individual achieve inner harmony; that art alone can elevate him above the life of society; and that the enjoyment of beauty creates for him special ethical criteria, different from those held by the crowd absorbed in the "low" affairs of practical existence.

Despite their friendship and the similarity of their philosophical, literary, and other interests, Tolstoy and Fet differed throughout the 1860's and 1870's in their attitude toward the beautiful and its place in life.

In contemplating nature, Fet never perceived any links between its power and beauty and the human conflicts of daily life. He discovered and revealed to others the way in which the simplest sensations can reveal the beautiful to man (sensations of sound, light, color; the contrast between heat and cold; even deceptive sights and sounds). Such sensations not only released in Fet mighty lyrical outpourings, but also turned his thoughts to profound reflections upon the principal problems of human existence—problems of love, life, and death. At all times he confined himself to the sensations and lyrical emotions of a single individual; he reflected on man and the world within the limits of a single human life apart from society.

Fet's friends Turgenev and Tolstoy adopted a different attitude toward nature. Boris Bukhshtab has pointed out the striking resemblance of the nature descriptions in Fet's "Kak zdes' svezho pod lipoiu gustoi" ("How Cool Beneath This Spreading Lime") and a passage from Turgenev's *Nakanune (On the Eve)*. Rejecting the possibility of Turgenev's having borrowed from Fet, Bukhshtab accepts the similarity of images, responses, and metaphors as an indication of the close affinity between the two writers.[7]

It seems to us that this resemblance, so subtly noted, may be attributed to the borrowing of certain details by one skillful landscape painter from another whom he implicitly trusted as a keen and exact observer. But the resemblance, though patent, must not blind us to equally obvious differences.

Fet's poem leads us to a perception of summer heat by means of contrasting the coolness in the shade of the lime tree with the blazing fields beyond, all this modulating into a wonderful sense of serenity evoked by nature's splendor at the height of summer.

The episode from the novel *On the Eve*, in which Turgenev presents a similar portrayal of nature, describes the searchings of two young people for a meaningful life and confirms through their sufferings and experiences the concept of struggle, self-sacrifice, and service to others as a source of human happiness. One of the novel's most important messages is that the idea of escape into the realm of pure art or science is narrow and inadequate.

In his story *Semeinoe schast'e (Family Happiness)*, Tolstoy also has a passage describing the contrast between the cool shade of the trees and the enervating heat of the open fields, and if he does not consciously challenge Fet's ideas, he at least gives frank expression to an esthetic attitude diametrically opposed to his: while Tolstoy's young heroine is enjoying the silence, the beauty, and the refreshing coolness offered by the canopy of the trees, she is suddenly struck with a sense of the injustice of her enjoying these privileges while the peasants are forced to work unprotected in the fierce heat of the sun.

In a letter of 1865 to Fet, in which he speaks of the beauty and prosperity in which his family lives, Tolstoy also contrasts their fate with that of the peasants. He is unable to shut himself up in the world of beauty and feel secure in it, even for a moment.

On our table we have red radishes, yellow butter, fresh, crisp-crusted bread on a pure white cloth, the garden is green, our young ladies are decked out in fine muslin, rejoicing in the heat and the shade, while that devil drought is having his way, sowing the fields with weeds, causing the parched earth to split open, lacerating the calloused heels of the peasants and their women, cracking the cattle's hooves, and it will give them all such a shaking up that we in our muslin frocks in the shade of our lime trees . . . will surely be made to feel it.[8]

Fet reminded him again and again of art and kept trying to lure him into the sphere of pure creative activity, above and beyond all distracting thoughts. "Ah, Lev Nikolaevich, try, if you can, to open the window into the world of art. That is where paradise is to be found, that is where objects can be the ideal."[9]

One must not, however, conclude that the ideal objects of which Fet wrote Tolstoy were abstract objects, mere philosophical conceptions. In his opinion, the world of art is an ideal world where every object achieves a state of perfection and expresses its essence and its harmonious relationship with all other phenomena without sacrificing its living objectivity, reality, form.

Art is to reality as a copy is to the object copied; the copy lives its own life, similar to the life of the original, but different from it and independent of it. Fet's concept was the following, although he would not, of course, have expressed it in such terms: "Poetry, and indeed all art, is the representation not of

an object but of the ideal of an object; the representation of
the object itself would be not only undesirable but even impossible." Only one aspect of an object is of importance to the
artist, Fet asserted—its beauty. Beauty is an attribute of all
things, of all objects, of everything that exists, not only in the
world, but in the universe. The subjective aspect of art Fet
found in the artist's penetration, his ability to perceive the
beautiful. "Since the world is equally beautiful in all its manifestations, it makes no difference what external things the poet
chooses for representation. Everything depends on the other,
the inner element—the sharpness of the poet's insight, the
strength of his clairvoyance."[10]

On the basis of these principles it has been justly assumed
that Fet's system of esthetics has much in common with Im-
pressionism.[11] It is true that for him the impression, the emotional response, was of more importance than the objective
attributes of the thing contemplated. Yet it is the objective
world that furnishes the poet with impressions and emotional
responses, and it is this world that he perceives and to which
he accords lyrical significance in his verse. Fet found the
richest, most objective poetic perception to be that which was
most logical and most capable of uniting human beings, of
creating ties binding them together. Art is capable of trans-
mitting the impressions of one individual to other individuals,
of "infecting" one person with the emotions of another, of
merging the individual contemplating the world with the world
as he perceives it. Art converts man into an optical instrument
reflecting nature, and nature into a source of poetry for man.
Fet believed that poetry revealed the "secret kinship of nature
and the soul, perhaps even their identity."

Without denying the significance of thought in poetry, Fet
strictly limited reason's "rights." He distinguished between
logical thought and poetic thought, the difference between
them being intrinsic to the nature of each:

Philosophical ideas gain in quality from the precision of their expression, the limitations of the sphere to which they appertain, the
resemblance they bear to incontrovertible axioms. Poetic ideas, on the
contrary, however vivid and powerful, become the more poetic the

more general they are, the wider, more delicate and elusive the rings radiating from their impact. Unlike philosophical ideas, they are not intended to add to the vast edifice of human thought and form the basis for building further deductions; they are designed to illuminate the architectonic spaces of a work of art or to glow faintly, almost imperceptibly, in its depths.[12]

In short, Fet divorced poetry from philosophy and staunchly opposed the practice, which had taken deep root in the 1830's, of making lyrical verse the medium for conveying philosophical ideas.

That does not mean that Fet took no interest in philosophy. On the contrary, like all the members of the intelligentsia in his generation, he took great interest in it, especially in his youth before entering the literary arena, when he numbered among his best friends such philosophically inclined young men as Grigorev and Vvedensky. His poetry of the 1840's and 1850's, however, reflects this interest only indirectly, as the basis on which to apprehend nature and interpret her laws.

Participation in the heated discussions of esthetic problems, of which Tolstoy and Turgenev soon grew tired and abandoned, had important consequences for Fet. They revived his interest in philosophy and led him to plunge into a deep study of it, as a result of which he became engrossed in Schopenhauer's thought and began translating his works into Russian. Both Fet and his friend Tolstoy found themselves in sympathy with Schopenhauer's pessimistic views of the world and with Schopenhauer himself, who, of all the German idealistic philosophers, was the most poetic. The changes that occurred in Fet's private life at the end of the 1850's and the beginning of the 1860's also stimulated his interest in philosophy.

The success of the collection of 1856 induced Fet to devote himself primarily to literature. He worked in various genres, made translations from a number of languages, and was widely published. The military career he had chosen as a means of regaining his place among the hereditary nobility disappointed him: a new decree was issued, stipulating that only the rank of colonel could confer a hereditary title on an officer. Fet realized that he would never attain that rank. In 1857 he married Mariya Vasilevna Botkina, and in 1858 resigned from military service.

Fet's strong defense of "pure art" in discussions of esthetics and especially his articles "Notes on Free Labor" and "Village Life" (1862), in which, as the owner now of a country estate, he wrote as a conservative landlord defending his interests against the claims of the peasants, spoiled his reputation with readers and critics alike. A collection of his poems published in 1863 was received coolly by some critics, with hostility by others. His verse was looked upon as the realization of his esthetic views; the criticism of it was more or less damning, depending upon the extent of the critic's objection to these views. Even such a reserved critic as Saltykov-Shchedrin, who sought to remain objective in his appraisal of Fet's poetry, declared in no uncertain terms that the themes of his poems were too slight and insignificant to win for him any but the most humble place in literature.

The poet became the butt of satire on the pages of the democratic journal *Iskra* (*The Spark*). Humorists of the 1860's delighted in lampooning him. Endless comic effects were suggested by the situation of this refined, lyric poet who, while urging others to take refuge from the low pursuits of daily life in pure art, was at the same time a shrewd landowner, jealously guarding his own interests and seeking his own profit.

Realizing that his literary career was over, Fet threw himself into the management of his estate and refused to publish any more poetry. The study of Schopenhauer's philosophy reconciled him to the ambiguity of his life. He found himself in complete sympathy with Schopenhauer's pessimism, his lack of faith in historical progress, and his reverence for art as a sphere safe from the devastating intrusions of the will and the instinct of self-preservation. Schopenhauer's theories confirmed Fet's views on art and society and strengthened his conviction that he was in the right.[13]

Fet's acceptance of Schopenhauer's philosophy is not surprising when we recall that his philosophical leanings had been determined by earlier readings of Kant and Schelling, thinkers who in many respects anticipated Schopenhauer. For many years Fet worked over the translation of Schopenhauer's *The*

World as Will and Idea, which was published in 1881. One
of Fet's favorite tenets borrowed from the great German thinker
and emphatically reiterated by the poet was that deliberate
logical thought is inimical to a work of art; yet it was with
the final elaboration of his antirational esthetic system that
Fet began to express logical philosophical ideas in his poetry.
His first philosophical poems, anticipating and preparing the
way for his later lyrics, dealt with the nature of art; they were
polemical poems directed against rationalism and in support
of "the bard's mad whims."

II   *Poems about Poetry*

As early as 1854, Fet wrote his "Muza" ("To My Muse"),
which was included in the collection of 1856. While gazing
into the heart of his own muse, Fet could not resist a backward
glance at Pushkin's celebrated poem of the same title. The
difference between the two stands out clearly against the background of a severe anthological style. Pushkin's muse is bright
and clear, one that would most appeal to the heart and mind
of the childlike poet, whereas Fet's lacks such harmony. His
muse is secret, and bears in her heart the sorrow and unfulfilled
dreams that foreshadow his future break with the world:

> Her head divine was all encircled by a braid
> Most intricately woven of scented golden strands;
> The year's last blooms were quivering in her hands;
> Impulsive her speech, and laden with a weight of sorrow,
> And woman's whims and wiles, and silver-tinted dreams,
> Sufferings indescribable, and unaccountable tears.
> Under the heavy spell of languor
> I listened till I heard, mingling with the words,
> A kiss. When she was gone my soul was sick for long
> And I was haunted by a yearning undefined.   (266–67)

Fet's irrational muse with her inexplicable fancies and her
inability to explain her sufferings and tears symbolizes a world
outlook opposite to that held by Pushkin, who cried: "Hail to
the Muse! Hail to Reason!"[14]

Fet's muse of 1854 is even more decidedly in conflict with

Nekrasov's. The latter's poem of the same name exactly resembles Fet's in formal composition, but while Nekrasov devotes the first half to drawing a contrast between his muse of "wrath and sorrow" and the serenely beautiful muses of anthological poetry, and the second half to a declaration of the social and humanitarian nature of the songs his muse inspires in him, Fet devotes the first half of his poem to a denunciation of social heroics in poetry, and the second half to presenting as the ideal the psychological lyric depicting the most subtle movements of the human heart.

In propounding his poetic system and defending his muse, Fet goes no further than to defend his artistic identity, define its peculiarities, distinguish his manner from that of other poets who have won recognition, and assert his right to originality. He does not denounce other systems or declare them beyond the pale of art. Although he contends that the social muse, who is sure to bring her protégé public laurels, is vainglorious, she is none the less a muse and one capable of inspiring high poetry. She is, however, alien in spirit to all of Fet's poetic aspirations, and he writes of her: "My ear is not caressed by her effective tongue, / Simple and adroit, uttering chords without accord" (266).

This poem, while unambiguous, is thus innocent of the spirit of exclusivity. It is not a philosophical tract dedicated to a theoretical analysis of problems of esthetics. It is simply a presentation in imagery and metaphor of the poet's individual artistic method.

It should be noted that Fet describes his muse as breathing the air of simplicity—human, "domestic" simplicity. This first conception of his muse, which appeared in the *Lyrical Pantheon,* was preserved throughout the years, later to merge oddly with an image of her as an all-powerful goddess reigning over the world. In the version of "To My Muse" written in 1857 and published in Nekrasov's *Contemporary* in 1858, the intimate picture of her as friend and sister to the poet still prevails:

And have you come to sit with me for long,
And force me to love and agonize again?
And whose, I pray, the image you have this time borrowed?

And whose the gentle phrases your cunning has acquired?
Well, your hand. Sit down. Now light the torch of inspiration
And sing, my kindly visitor! ...   (275)

Although later in the poem he speaks of leaving this world
of art and even introduces into his text a phrase from Pushkin's
"The Mob" which often served as a weapon in the hands of
champions of pure art in the discussions of the 1850's (Pushkin:
"Not for the welter of daily living ... were we born ..."; Fet:
"Putting behind us the welter of daily living / We feed the
flame of life with purest dreams ..."), still this poem cannot
be considered a declaration of the poet's platform.

Quite different is the message Fet dispatched to Turgenev
in 1865, a "Horatian" message sent by a poet-recluse who has
sought solitude in the lap of nature. Here we can see Fet's
intolerance undisguised, his determined rejection of all liberal,
"rebellious" literature, his insistence on seeing in Turgenev's
fate corroboration of his conviction that those who would serve
the muse must necessarily eschew interest in contemporary
affairs, and his effort to enlist Pushkin as a supporter of his
stand:

> Of mast and sail (how honestly they served
> The skillful swimmer in the wind and storm!)
> You fashioned for yourself an aerial dwellingplace
> Beneath a cliff enchanted.
>
> The radiance of an alien dawn did bid you welcome,
> And in your words we hear a note of resignation.   (483)

The image of the bard cast upon the shore and finding
shelter under a cliff can undoubtedly be traced to Pushkin's
"Arion," but Pushkin's poet sings "hymns of a former day"
while Fet's, in lonely solitude, seeks "his soul's renascence."
The ideas behind the similar images are not only dissimilar,
they are antithetical. Fet distorts Pushkin's images to suit his
needs again, further on, when he makes allusions to Pushkin's
"The Village" (Pushkin: "Your joyful voice is better heard in
this majestic solitude"; Fet: "The muse's tender notes here sound
more clearly"). But if Pushkin concludes his poetic description

of village and countryside by having the "friend of mankind" appeal to the social conscience and sense of civic responsibility, Fet ends with "It is done! My door is shut against the evil weather!" and demonstratively refuses to participate in any form of social action. Turgenev, author of *Fathers and Sons,* who at that time was preparing to write *Smoke,* did not look favorably upon this message. He was living abroad for purely personal reasons, and he did not wish this to be interpreted as an "escape" from anything at all. He was not filled with the spirit of resignation; nor, apparently, was Fet, who angrily wrote of the "filthy debauchery" of "ignoramuses." In this message, he made no secret of the dreary thoughts prompted by his withdrawal to a life of seclusion in the country, but his confession elicited only irony from Turgenev, who told him he had better return to the city if country life filled him with thoughts of death. In spirit and tone, Fet's message to Turgenev was a foretaste of the splenetic outbursts in defense of his esthetic views that turned into political attacks and, especially in the epigrams, assumed the form of vicious insinuations—"Psevdo-poetu" ("To a Pseudo-Poet"); "Poniaten zov tvoi serdobol'nyi" ("Your Compassionate Appeal"); "Ne tolkui ob obez'iane" ("Consider Not the Monkey"); and others.

Happily, the number of instances in which Fet resorted to this means of defending his views—which invariably shocked and repelled his contemporaries—was inconsequential in comparison with the stream of philosophical verse, so different in tone, which he produced at the same time.

The philosophical lyrics of the 1860's to the 1880's violated the principle to which he had adhered so staunchly in the first twenty years of his writing, namely, that it was through images rather than ideas that poetry is to be expressed. His new verse was full of philosophical reflections, and enlisted metaphor and simile in the service of the abstract idea. Many of the works of these years were presented as soliloquies revealing the emergence of the idea and offering it, not in finished form, but as thought-emotion, thought controlling the consciousness but not appearing in strict logical sequence.

His celebrated "Kak beden nash iazyk" ("How Poor Is Human Speech!") belongs to this group of reflective poems.

There can be no question as to what the poet wished to say: language is inadequate for the expression of feeling, and knowledge cannot come to its assistance (first stanza); only inspired art can do this (second stanza). In other words, the thought of the poem is clear and rational. Little does it resemble the "unconscious murmurings of sleep" (a metaphor which Turgenev attributed to Fet): the poet proves capable of lucidly conveying his idea to the reader. Where does the irrationalism of this particular poem lie—the irrationalism that Fet considered basic to his poetry and that was recognized by his contemporaries as well as by students of his work down to our own day? First of all, it lies in the manner in which the idea is expressed. Fet's emphasis is placed not on the idea itself, but on the workings of the human mind that give birth to the idea. This poem represents a soliloquy, a chain of reflections, only a few of which are carried to a logical conclusion and given finished form; the rest fade away in the depths of consciousness, are hidden, as it were, in a forest of associations. Let us consider the first stanza:

How poor is human speech!—I would and yet I cannot—
No, not to friend or foe can I impart
Knowledge of this clear wave that surges in my heart.
In vain this anguished striving:
Before the fatal falsehood
A very Solomon must bow his head. (308–309)

"How poor is human speech!"—this opening exclamation lends itself to many interpretations and suggests a number of questions, the first of which is: why should a poet speak of the poverty of human speech? The innumerable answers to this brief and noncommittal exclamation offer rich fields of exploration. The second half of the line assists the reader in orienting himself. The poet speaks of the poverty of language because he is frustrated—but in what way? The second sentence is as obscure as the first. The first was at least colored by emotion; the second, fenced in by dashes and consisting of two subjects and two incomplete predicates, is clearly a tattered thought. Its fragmentary character and its "hardening" (the dashes suggest the rupture of logical development) indicate the speaker's inarticulateness and his refusal to try to find means of communicating his thought. Then comes another outburst of emotion: "Not to friend or foe can I impart / Knowledge of this clear wave that surges in my heart." In this extended sentence we find a semblance of logic. The poet tells us he has lost faith in the possibility of imparting his feelings to others. Yet we do not yet know what direction his further reflections will take: will we be told what feelings are surging in his breast? Will we learn who his friends and foes are and be informed of his efforts to discover sounds in the language corresponding to his feelings? He omits all this and leaps directly from a brief and turbulent statement of his mood to a pessimistic conclusion: "In vain this anguished striving." The comprehensiveness of this summation allows us to supply not one but many logical links with the thoughts preceding it and to postulate many ways of developing the idea. Fet, however chooses an unexpected course. Despairing of finding adequate words to express himself in language and convinced of the accumulation of century-old and inescapable misunderstandings ("fatal falsehood"), he declares: "Before the fatal falsehood / A very Solomon must bow his head."

The second stanza, the antiphony, asserts it is given to poetry to express that which confounds ordinary language and knowledge:

> For you alone, oh poet, the wingèd word
> Seizes in flight and suddenly affixes
> The dark delirium of the soul, the herb's elusive scent;
> So Jupiter's eagle, scorning the narrow valley,
> Rises to the sky's unfenced immensity,
> Clutching in its claws a sheaf of streakèd lightning. (309)

Here we have no fragmentary sentences whose logic collapses and whose parts are linked only by association. What the poet says is couched in the free language of poetry rather than in the brittle forms of ordinary speech. In one long, flowing period it embraces three couplets and is crowned by a mighty metaphor. Its composition is governed not by "the bard's mad whims" but by a strict and consistent organization of material shaped to the fullest expression of the idea. The "inexpressible" content suggested in the first stanza is given expression in the second, where the poet seems to regain his powers of articulation. The content is "The dark delirium of the soul, the herb's elusive scent,"—in other words, the unconscious workings of the mind and the beauty of nature, accessible to man only through sensual perception. The metaphor at the end of the poem, typical of Fet's thinking, violates the literary cliché: instead of Jupiter's eagle bringing the lightning of artistic inspiration down to earth, it rises from earth into the heaven of poetry, carrying in its claws the lightning of earthly impressions. The poem "Lastochki" ("Swallows") has a similar ending. In this poem, likening the poet's daring to the bird's, Fet writes:

> Up it soars, a streak upon the blue,
> And one trembles lest the sky
> Close upon the bold intruder
> And tear to shreds its wings of lightning. . . .
>
> And do not I, a humble vessel,
> Thrust into forbidden wells,
> Hoping to scoop if but one drop
> Of freshness from their depths?   (108)

The forbidden depths, accessible only to the poet, are to be found, according to Fet, not beyond reality as the Romantics assumed, but in the innermost recesses of life. Those blessed with creative powers can discover the treasures in these depths and elevate them to the sphere of art.

Even in verse dealing with abstract concepts, Fet's principal purpose remained the contemplation of psychological processes, while his imagery was derived from his observation of ever-changing, ever-moving, natural phenomena. It is this characteristic that distinguishes his meditative poems from the philosophical lyrics of Baratynsky and Tyutchev.

III   Poems about Music

In Fet's poems about music we find a combination of psychological analysis and esthetic reflection. Because art does not impose laws of human logic upon life and does not destroy the living image of an object, Fet placed art above learning; and of all the forms of art he ranked music the highest, as the art most independent of logic.

As early as the 1840's, Fet declared his dissatisfaction with language as a medium for expressing emotion. He longed to supplement the language of words with some other language, and of all these he found the musical idiom the richest and most direct. It was his dream to "speak without words," to speak "with the soul"; he did, in fact, reinforce the semantic aspect of words with associative and carefully selected tone values. The significance of individual sounds and of combinations of sounds was as important to him as the stress and melody of a line, and every one of his verses is a complex tonal composition accompanying, and often supplementing, the meaning of the words.[15] This facet of Fet's work was reflected in his theoretical esthetic views, and he himself attached great importance to it.

The attempt to supplement the word with sound, with music, and constantly to invent new forms of auditory expressiveness by varying rhythm, measure, orchestration, and the intonational construction of a sentence, resulted in his attempting to convey music in words, in verbal imagery. One of his finest poems of this kind is "Pevitse" ("The Singer"; 1857), in which, in addition to the musical pattern of the verse, the curious interweaving of fragments of scenery with emotions reproduces the flow of images that pass through the mind while one is listening to music.

> Oh, sweep my heart up into singing spaces
>   Where sorrow is poised like the moon o'er the wood;
> In those heavenly sounds love is smiling shyly
>   To solace your burning tears.
>
> How easily, child, 'mid invisible waves,
>   I give myself up to your song,
> To be carried aloft along silvery paths,
>   A pale ghost in the wake of a wing.
>
> In the distance your voice is expiring, agleam
>   Like the sea as the sun goes down,

And I hear, though I know not whence it comes,
A sudden strewing of pearls.

Oh, sweep my heart up into singing spaces
Where sorrow smiles shyly as love.
Ever higher I mount the silvery path,
A pale ghost in the wake of a wing. (182)

The images and emotions are born of the music and the
fantastic picture that results is the music's visual image.[16] In
the poet's mind, the world of music is juxtaposed to the real
world about him, thereby forming a new reality in which
objects and feelings exist on an equal plane and intermingle
freely. This world, created by sounds and dependent exclusively
upon sounds, has its own spaces—"singing spaces"—with the
sky above, earth and sea beneath. It exists, as it were, beyond
time, since it lasts only as long as the music, but there is a
logical succession of events, for the sunset fades and the moon
rises and illumines the waters of the bay.

Music frees man from earthly ties—first of all, from the tie
of gravity. He lives a double life. While listening to music he
shares the life of the music, becomes part of its world. Sub-
mitting to its laws, he leaves the earth and soars into the
heaven of poetry, "a pale ghost in the wake of a wing," through
spaces belonging to song alone. The sky lighted by the rising
moon, the earth rimmed by woods, the sea with the sunset
fading on the horizon—this is the vision evoked by the music.
The very spaces of the world of music arise from a sense of
flight engendered by the peace and freedom the music brings,
and the moonlit landscape is created by sounds associated
with silver and moonlight (silvery tone, rings of silver, silver
bells—things related to the color of silver, which in its turn
suggests silvery light, moonlight—this is the order of association
common to the Russian language, its folklore, and its poetry).

The scenery of the world of music is constructed of objects
and phenomena familiar to the poet in the real world: the
limitless spaces above—the sky; the limitless spaces below—the
sea; as well as the vast earth, bounded on the horizon by the
forest, which Fet, true to his love of the intimate and concrete,
diminishes to "woods." Yet all these "real" elements furnishing

the musical spaces are but images represénting emotions: resigned, meek sorrow; hot tears; lofty love; mutual trust; and the joy of communion.

The joy and sorrow of both poet and singer, whose souls merge in the moment of ecstasy, become identified with the moon above the woods, rays of moonlight, and the sun sinking into the sea.

All the feelings and images of this poem are about music. The conjunction of sorrow and a smile—the minor key "illuminated" by the major—the sunset on the sea, the voice fading away, only to burst forth into a coloratura run like the "strewing of pearls." The evening scene is dictated by a sense of silence, since the ear is entirely absorbed by the music. Variations on the theme of flight, moonlight, tears and a smile, parallel the development of the musical phrase in a song.

The imagery of music is repeated in a later poem, "Shopenu" ("To Chopin"; 1882). Although the poem is dedicated to the great Polish composer, it is neither about him nor about a performance of his music. It is instead a lyric celebrating the undying power of love, presented in images arising from Chopin's music.

The musical structure of the poem is that of a mazurka, light and quick in tempo, with a precise yet shifting rhythmic pattern.

Curiously enough, the visual imagery evoked in Fet by Chopin's music closely resembles that perceived by the eminent Russian choreographer Michel Fokine when he staged his ballet "The Sylphs," based on Chopin's music. This similarity would seem to indicate that such imagery is not a purely subjective phenomenon.

The poet's dead love appears to him in gauzelike garments, dancing lightly. The magic of the music enables the poet easily and joyfully to escape the bonds of time and slip back to the hour when they were together. Time now obeys new laws, whereby the past becomes the present and the present the future; but this future never arrives, since the end of the music brings an end to time and the poet's heart stops beating when the dance is over.

Swift you entered, lightly, blithely,
Set my heart to beating wildly;
'Neath the magic of the music
Rise old raptures, rise old tortures.
Now I feel your trembling fingers—
    You are with me still!

Hour of triumph, hour of mourning!
Hour of ending, hour of parting!
There you stand, your lashes lowered,
Wearing still that gauzy garment.
Hope may die—shall I regret it
    Once this hour is mine?

Now your hand my hand is touching,
Once again my heartbeats quicken;
Nevermore to wretched grieving
Shall I turn as I was wont to;
Now to all am I indifferent—
    Dead my fire and cold.

All the world is held in bondage
By the music's magic power;
Let my anguished heart be given
Wholly to this hour of parting;
When the music sounds no longer,
    Beats no more this heart.   (193)

Fet was not alone among his contemporaries in seeking a union of poetry and music. Leo Tolstoy, in whose life music played such an important part, made a similar effort to depict in literature the individual's response to music—in particular, to singing—by means of a stream of thoughts and feelings which, in their turn, give rise to visual images ("Albert," *War and Peace*).

Musicians have noted Fet's success in heightening the impact of words and phrases by supplementing their logical meaning by the emotional effect of sound. This explains why so many composers of Fet's day chose his lyrics to set to music: the songs thus produced achieved a wide popularity that persisted even after Fet had lost his hold on the reading public.

In Tchaikovsky's setting of "The Singer," the composer gives his own interpretation of what the singer, a woman, sang to Fet. In a letter to Grand Duke Konstantin Konstantinovich (who signed his own poems with the initials, K. R. [Konstantin Romanov]), Tchaikovsky wrote:

Fet is an exceptional phenomenon in literature; he is not to be compared with even the best poets, here or abroad.... In his finest moments he goes beyond the bounds of poetry and steps boldly into our sphere. At times, Fet reminds me of Beethoven, never of Pushkin, Goethe, Byron or Musset. Like Beethoven, he is capable of touching heart strings inaccessible to poets, great as they may be, who are limited to words. He is not just a poet, rather a poet-musician, who rejects themes that lend themselves too easily to verbal expression. For that reason he is often misunderstood; indeed, there are certain gentlemen who laugh at him and find poems such as "Oh, sweep my heart up into singing spaces" sheer nonsense—as no doubt it is for such uncultivated and unmusical gentlemen.... [17]

Without taking Tchaikovsky's words about Fet's going "beyond the bounds of poetry" too literally, we must note that Fet provided great impetus to the further development of poetry by making the melodic and euphonic pattern more intricate and placing more emphasis on this aspect of a poem. Fet was well acquainted with Russian vocal music: in his youth, he had absorbed the musical intonations of Russian drawingroom and folk songs as well as gypsy songs. This circumstance is often reflected in his verse. One of Fet's contributions to literature was the growth in relative importance of "song lyrics" in Russian poetry of the middle of the nineteenth century.[18]

At the same time, he and his contemporaries—for instance, Yakov Polonsky, Aleksey Tolstoy, and Lev Mey—aided the development of vocal music by enriching its themes and intonational structure.

CHAPTER 5

Last Years

I *From the Collection of 1856 to* Evening Lights

FET'S two-volume collection of 1863 was more like a summation of the life work of a poet about to conclude his creative activities than the latest offering of a poet regularly contributing to current journals and providing his readers with his most recent writing. In the preface to the collection of 1856, his publishers justified the inclusion of poems from the 1850 edition by asserting they had been heavily revised, intimating that the preceding edition had been carelessly prepared. In the preface to the 1863 edition, Fet himself stated that "only one item appertaining to my old work . . . is included,"[1] and that the texts of poems from the 1856 edition had not been revised. To these former poems were added those written after 1856.

The second half of the edition consisted of translations of foreign poets, including Horace, Ovid, Catullus, Hafiz, Goethe, Schiller, Mickiewicz, André Chénier, and Heine. This section of the edition reveals Fet as a serious scholar interested in the poetry of various times and peoples, beginning with antiquity and ending with contemporary Germany, France, and Poland. Not only did he investigate the work of individual poets (making a particularly thorough study of Horace), but he also discovered for himself the distinguishing characteristics of the poetry of various countries. There is good reason to assume that he pondered upon the lives of his predecessors, comparing their fate with his own and drawing conclusions from those comparisons. In his introduction to his translations of Horace he remarks: "Horace's relations with his patron Maecenas and at one time with Augustus were as delicate as they were brief, . . . as witnessed by the fact that despite offers of wealth and

126

fame, our poet satisfied himself with a minimum of comfort all his life and, as a Stoic, took pride in this."[2] We are reminded that in Fet's relations with the Czar's family, to whom he later became closely attached, he too sought to preserve a "delicate" independence, but did not always succeed[3] (nor did Horace, for that matter).

Fet also speaks of Horace's devotion to Cinara, who died young (a devotion contrasting with the superficial attitude toward love that Horace assumed in his writing); and of the enormous influence exerted upon his personality and esthetic ideals by the scenery of the province in which he was born; and by his living in the country, when his creative activities were at their height. "As an ardent admirer of nature endowed with the artistic gift of perceiving her most secret beauties, he [Horace] was ever one who yearned for a life of peace and rural quietude,"[4] wrote Fet, paraphrasing Pushkin's *Eugene Onegin* ("Born was I for a life of peace and rural quietude"). Surely, in writing these words, Fet also had himself in mind, and his own attitude toward nature and country life.

In his introduction to his translations of Hafiz, Fet presents the Persian poet as one who in old age renounced mysticism and the ascetic life to become the singer of love and the joys of this world. His knowledge of Hafiz, gleaned from an article by the German poet Georg Friedrich Daumer,[5] may very well have exerted a strong influence upon him when, in his own old age, he wrote erotic poetry and verse testifying to his insatiable love of life.

In the first volume of the 1863 edition, the poetry is grouped according to the same cycles as in 1856, with the addition of two new ones: "The Sea" and "Spring." These two were placed just before the final section, "Miscellany," and in no way changed the basic structure of the book. The poems for the new cycles were taken largely from the old "Miscellany," augmented by new verse. All the other cycles were likewise augmented.

Fet declared that he had brought out the edition of 1863 because the 1856 collection was out of print. This would seem to indicate that he enjoyed the approval of at least part of the reading public—that, as he put it, "his Muse was not without kind friends." The 1863 collection failed to corroborate this, for it did not sell out in his lifetime. Nor did it receive favorable reviews in *The Contemporary, The Russian Word, Notes of the Fatherland* or *Library for Reading.* Most of the journals received it not just coldly, but with hostility.

In the 1860's and 1870's, Fet lived on his estate, "Stepanovka," in the Mtsensk district, on rare occasions making trips to Moscow. He wrote little verse, and what he did write he sent first to Leo Tolstoy, according to his old custom of seeking the opinion of his literary friends. In 1874 the friendship between Fet and Turgenev ended in a bitter quarrel arising from their different viewpoints. There is every reason to believe that Turgenev's persistent denunciation of all of Fet's later poetry, his advice to Fet to stop writing verse, his jokes and sarcasms in letters to friends about the sour fermenting of the poet's "wounded and bottled-up literary vanity,"[6] had the effect of further injuring Fet and intensifying the wrath with which he inveighed against the political liberalism and radicalism upon which Turgenev staked his hopes.

In contrast to Turgenev, who felt little sympathy for his friend at a time when he was undergoing a crisis in his creative life, Tolstoy encouraged Fet, praised his poems and tried to convince him that his powers were not exhausted (see Tolstoy's letter to Fet of June 28, 1867). He himself sought the poet's support for his writings, asked him for his opinions, and valued them highly.

Fet was one of the first of Tolstoy's acquaintances to appreciate the depth and significance of *Anna Karenina* and to support and inspire the writer during his work on that novel.

Turgenev saw in the Fet of those years a "finished" poet, one who had "written himself out." This impression was based on the belief that that particular historical period had no use for poetry, not even to the extent of battling "pure" poetry by lampooning poets who wrote of love and nature or indulged in lyrical philosophizing.[7]

Even at the time when Turgenev still admired Fet's poetry, he had no sympathy with the poet's use of it as a medium for expressing his Romantic philosophy. This view he expressed clearly while preparing the 1856 collection. On the margin of

"Stay. How Fair This Spot!" he wrote: "Marvelous! This poem can be made into a jewel if we begin with a description of the quiet night and end with the line "I will not go there"; but all this pious star-gazing—the devil with it!"[8]

Turgenev failed to note Fet's tendency to deepen the philosophical trend of his lyrics. Tolstoy, on the other hand, who considered Fet one of the most able thinkers among his acquaintances[9] and who first suggested to Fet that he translate Schopenhauer, instantly saw and approved of this. Although Tolstoy was deeply moved by Fet's poems "in the old manner," he was convinced that the poet's aspirations for the future should be concentrated on the development of his philosophical lyrics.

When Fet sent Tolstoy his poem "Sredi zviozd" ("Among the Stars"; 1876), Tolstoy replied: "Not only is this poem worthy of you, it is particularly, yes, particularly good because of its poetical-philosophical nature, which is only what I expected of you."

Tolstoy went on to elaborate on his high opinion of the poem, adding to his own opinion that of Nikolay Strakhov, a critic, philosopher and Slavophile who was to become Fet's friend and adviser. "Strakhov paid us a visit during the holidays and . . . we often recalled you, your words and thoughts and verse. I read to him the poem you sent me in your last letter—'Among the Stars'—and he was as delighted as I was . . . It is one of the finest poems I know."[10]

The mood, the philosophical problems touched upon, even the imagery of some of Fet's poems remind us of Tolstoy, and this is only natural, for they reflect the same philosophical searchings which occupied Tolstoy at the time.

In the works of both Fet and Tolstoy, the sky, which in *War and Peace* Tolstoy uses to suggest the idea of eternity, becomes the symbol of the universal, the eternal and unchanging, all that is above and beyond human life.

As early as 1857, Fet expressed his sense of the opposition of man and the universe, and the ecstatic experience of being freed of earthly bonds and merging with the universe, if but for a brief moment. For Fet this experience was associated with special and concrete circumstances:

One Southern night I lonely lay
On a stack of hay, my face upturned
To where the glowing constellations
Sang and circled in the sky.

The poet, as we see from the verse, was lying on an elevation
and gazing into the Southern night sky, particularly dark and
with particularly bright stars—usual in the South, but very
striking for a Northerner, accustomed to less brilliant night
skies. In such a situation, the poet was overwhelmed by a
sense of his closeness to, and helplessness in the face of, the
universe:

The earth, a vague and silent dream,
Anonymously whirled away,
And I, like Adam in the garden,
First looked upon the face of night.
Was it I who plunged into those spaces,
Or did the stars come seeking me?
With beating heart, with bated breath,
I measured with my eye those depths
In which, with every passing moment,
I more irrevocably sank.

Our contemporaries, who have seen the birth of space flight,
might recognize in this poem Fet's foretaste of what man
experiences when he overcomes the force of gravity and enters
the cosmos. Fet naturally had no such thought in mind. He
was awed and at the same time enraptured by his sense of
the infinity of space. With precision and inspiration he conveyed his feelings and the significance of these feelings without
revealing the root of the significance or the source of the feeling.

The precision with which Fet conveyed his feelings indicates
that the poet—"nature's spokesman," as he termed himself—had
achieved, by the power of his imagination, a feeling of weight-
lessness and of the absence of "top and bottom" in outer space.
What began as a flight into the sky ended as a plunge into
the void.

The poem Tolstoy so admired, "Among the Stars," written
nineteen years later, is quite different in character. It represents

a philosophical meditation on the beauty of the eternal, starry skies. In this verse the poet is not engaged either in self-contemplation or contemplation of nature. Here, the sky is not a real, if mysterious, part of nature, but a wellspring of ideas, forever evoking in man thoughts and feelings of a specific kind. The poet rejects all but one influence of the night skies: their influence on his thinking, his attitude toward his earthly existence. The poet knows that the stars move according to laws, and in that respect they are no more free than man. But he dismisses this thought. He is not interested in the knowledge of the stars gleaned by science. For him, they are the eternal symbol of poetry, the ever-present, visual incarnation of man's dream of immortality, infinity, and undying day.

> Whirl on, bondsmen, like me, of the passing moment,
> Slaves, like me, of the numbers governing our birth.
> Yet when I leaf the pages of the burning book
> It is no tale of numbers that I read.
>
> Like caliphs decked in wreaths, in rays, in diamonds,
> Incongruous among earth's sordid needs,
> You, dream undying of the hieroglyphics,
> Affirm: "We are forever; you—but for a day.
>
> We know no numbers. In vain with ravenous thinking
> You stalk the shadow of eternal thought.
> We shine here that in your deepest darkness
> Our constant day will seek admittance at your door.
>
> And that is why, when life is too oppressive,
> You gladly lift your harassed face from earth,
> Where all is dark and dreary, to gaze at us,
> Into our depths, where all is light and splendor."   (97)

Here, too, the sky is space, but its relation to the earth (the sky above, the earth below) is definite and inviolable. It is beyond the poet's reach. He is tragically doomed to a life on earth—a dull, petty life, whose needs make the splendor of the stars "incongruous." According to the poem, their significance lies in their being the antithesis of worldly life, so that when man raises his eyes to them, his opposite in space and essence, they offer him moral support in overcoming his sufferings and a criterion for measuring the vanity of earthly life. The sky is not the vault of heaven that can be seen in the North or the South, in summer or winter, but Kant's starry sky, the visual symbol of moral law.

In this poem we find the image of the starry sky presented in the traditional form used by many poets before Fet, including Lermontov and Heine. The freshness of Fet's approach lies not in his merely making use of this tradition, but presenting it as the central theme of his poem. Accepting this "eternal" symbol of poetry and philosophy, he considers how it came to be such a symbol, and turns philosophical observations on the relationship of man to the cosmos into a lyrical interpretation of the laws of poetry.

In many of Fet's poems of the 1870's and 1880's we find direct references to Schopenhauer's philosophy. The fourth stanza of the poem "Nichtozhestvo" ("Nothingness") is only a resetting of the idea from Part II, Chapter 41 of his *The World as Will and Idea*. Schopenhauer's influence is to be found in other poems as well,[11] but it is the combination of the ideas borrowed from Fet's favorite philosopher of those years with the themes that agitated him all his life, such as the theme of eternity and the passing moment, love and death, struggle and creative activity, that lend originality to the content of Fet's verse of the 1870's and 1880's.

The merging of lyrical and philosophical themes, the use of corresponding imagery and the development of a new poetic style made it possible for Fet to bring out a new book in the 1870's that was not simply another collection of verse, but a book of poetry whose unity was emphasized by the title. For the first time since youthful enthusiasm led him to call his first book the *Lyrical Pantheon*, he gave a name to his work. By titling this book, which contained poems written over a period of twenty years, *Vechernie ogni* (*Evening Lights*), Fet presented himself as an old man facing the eternal night ahead of him, lighting tapers of poetry to illumine, if but faintly, the gloom of his lonely and sorrowful existence.

The name not only set a lyrical tone of melancholy and introspection, not only intimated the lyrical and philosophical themes of the poems (Turgenev called the lyrical miniatures of his last years "Senilia"), it also served as a kind of musical key, so that the reader might attune himself to the verse.

As distinguished from all of Fet's former collections, this book contained no poems that had appeared before. Since Fet was sixty-four years old when it appeared, he no doubt looked upon it as the last collection to be published in his lifetime. As a matter of fact, he selected and published three more collections, which he called the second, third, and fourth editions of *Evening Lights,* in 1885, 1888, and 1891 respectively. Although the editions of these books were very small and sold quite badly, and although the poet constantly complained of his loneliness, he achieved at the end of his life the practical aims he had set himself. He became a wealthy man and was accepted as a member of the titled nobility. He was flattered by the friendship of young poets, especially Vladimir Solovev and Konstantin Romanov, who were attracted by the new philosophical style which in some ways anticipated Symbolism. The desire for social distinction that goaded him all his life remained with him in old age and led him to obtain for himself, through influential friends, a position at the Czar's court.

Yet the main thing in his life was, after all, literary activity. One after another his translations appeared: Schopenhauer's *The Fourfold Root of the Principle of Sufficient Reason* (1885), and *The World as Will and Idea* (1888); Parts I and II of Goethe's *Faust*; Virgil's *Aeneid* (1887–88); and others.

Only in work did the writer find the peace of mind and spiritual serenity that neither riches, nor the achievement of his vain ambitions, nor the favorable reviews of his *Evening Lights* could bring.

In 1890, the seventy-year-old poet published his memoirs in two volumes as *Moi vospominaniia (My Recollections)*. Despite cruel attacks of asthma, he worked indefatigably. He wrote one more volume of memoirs, *Rannie gody moei zhizni (The Early Years)*, published posthumously in 1893, and made plans for a new and complete edition of his works. On November 21, 1892, Fet died from an attack of asthma following an unsuccessful attempt to commit suicide.

One is struck by the unity and originality of style, the range and intensity of emotion, the profundity of the lyrical experiences expressed in Fet's later poetry, and by the wonderful imagery he created until the very last months of his life. These poems testify to the meager satisfaction he derived from the prosperity he so determinedly sought from the first years of manhood to the last of old age. They show also how deeply he was affected by the conflicts, compromises and sufferings he underwent for their sake, and how he despised everything he achieved at such great sacrifice.

II   Evening Lights

Most critics of Fet's poetry (Eikhenbaum, Bukhshtab, Gromov, Gustafson) point out the parallelism of the poet's descriptions of man and nature. We have already considered the intricate evolution of Fet's conception of the relationship between man and nature, the main theme of his work. We know that in the 1840's, the first period of Fet's creative activity, throughout which the persona of his lyrics was an emotionally morbid young man, a Russian Hamlet, whose inner world harmonized with the grim Northern scenery, its stern beauty and mysterious spaces, the poet felt at one with his surroundings and was inspired by intense love of country. In the 1850's his work is dominated by anthological poems, the calm, detached, poetic ideal. The harmonious and reconciliatory force of this type of art, which holds the soul's turbulence in subjection and allies itself with ideas of eternal life and eternal movement in nature, brought classic clarity and artistic perfection to his poetry of those years. In drawing a contrast between the first and second periods of Fet's career, we must speak only of dominating tendencies, always remembering that such a division is relative, that both tendencies—the tendency to depict conflict in man and nature, and the tendency to sing the harmony of the universe—exist throughout his work, and that each serves as a background for the other.

At the end of the 1850's and in the 1860's, the "harmony" of the parallelism of "man and nature" begins to collapse. If, as in the first period, Fet depicted nature as developing through conflict similar to that conflict which determined the development of man's moral nature, and in the 1850's found harmony in nature merging with the harmony of the human spirit, in the last period he was aware of the divergence of man and nature. The harmony in nature only emphasized the discord in human life, for man longs to be beautiful and immortal like nature but is doomed to a life of struggle ending in death.

This sense of conflict deepens in Fet during the 1870's. More and more he gives himself up to thoughts of death, to the realization that the life process must come to an end. The consolation afforded him in the 1840's and 1850's by his theory of expanding man's limited time allotment by cramming transitional moments with vital content, no longer comes to his aid. He is left to face the agonizing mystery of annihilation, without consolation or support.

With characteristic stoicism, pride, and spirit Fet accepted the doubt and sense of tragedy that now overwhelmed him. Just as in a former time he had broken with society, had denounced the idea of historical progress, and had withdrawn to a life in the country devoted to the service of "pure art," so now he broke with nature, negated her right to rule over him, and declared the union of his mind with the universe.

Fet's spiritual crisis, distinctly reflected in his later poems, was shared by most intellectuals of the 1880's.

In Russia, the 1880's were a period of political reaction, attended by cruel government reprisals on the one hand and disillusionment as to the effectiveness of popular resistance and of all revolutionary political activities on the other.

At the same time, these were years of intense philosophical inquiry and of serious research in the fields of natural science, economics, and politics, as a result of which some individuals turned to Marxism, others to neo-Kantian philosophy, and still others to various forms of idealism, even mysticism.

In contrast to Tolstoy, who, having in those years reconsidered his attitude toward all matters affecting human existence, renounced the society in which he lived with its morals, and declared for self-improvement for the sake of serving others, Fet, who also tried to discover the meaning of life and the place of man in nature and the universe, was interested only in the individual.

In their discussions of problems vital to both of them, Tolstoy was shocked by Fet's pride and aggressive inflexibility. On January 20, 1873, Fet wrote to Tolstoy in connection with false rumors of Turgenev's death:

The other day I read the rumors of Turgenev's death. Can they be true? Never have I been able to understand his comparing death to a huge calf's-foot jelly. A door into the void; in a word, nirvana —that I can understand. But a meat jelly?[12] I suppose my door is not far away. I am afraid of a life of misery, I am not afraid of nothingness. I remember it. Not bad. Peaceful. Attila chopped off heads and I didn't mind. Diocletian burned Christians and I didn't turn a hair. But you are angry with me.

In his letter Fet is obviously pursuing an argument he had begun with his friend. He knows Tolstoy will be annoyed by his enlisting "lamentable" incidents from the history of civilization to support his skepticism.

In his reply, Tolstoy advanced objections that were serious and a matter of principle with him:

There is no point in joking about nirvana, to say nothing of losing one's temper. Nirvana is vastly more interesting (at least to me it is) than life, but I admit that, ponder this matter as I may, I can come to no other conclusion than that nirvana is—nothingness. I stand for only one thing—religious veneration—a horror of that nirvana. After all, there is nothing of more importance.[13]

Fet, however, refused to accord "religious veneration" to either death or nirvana. In a poem addressed to death, he defies it, fully aware of his right to do so since death is nothing, while he is a thinking creature armed with the irresistible logic of the human mind:

Though the moment come when on my head your hand shall fall,
And I be thus erased from off the list of living,
In my own court, so long as I have mind to judge,
We two are equals, and the triumph all is mine.

You still are subject to the workings of my will,
You are a shadow at my feet, a faceless phantom,

A thought my mind has conjured, nothing more,
The fragile plaything of my most uncheerful dreams.   (104)

In a letter to Fet of January 23, 1873, Tolstoy, brushing aside
Fet's logical criticism of religion, advances it as man's psychological defense against the ideas of death and annihilation.
He wrote: "The marvelous thing about religion is that it has
rendered this service [reconciliation to death] for so many
centuries to so many millions of people.... With such a task,
how can you demand that it be logical? It is an absurdity,
but the only absurdity among millions that serves this purpose.
Oh yes, there's something to be said for it!"[14]

Fet, who in the 1860's had declared against rationalism in
his opposition to the pragmatic course society was taking, who
had announced the superiority of instinct over reason and had
argued himself blue in the face in the attempt to prove to
Turgenev that art and logical thinking are not fellow-travellers,
now brought a whole arsenal of logical arguments to bear
against the instinctive, the "natural" fear of death, fortifying
his position by making Schopenhauer his ally.

Addressing nothingness—nirvana—he attempts to conquer the
awe it inspires in him by subjecting it to logical analysis:

Who art thou? And why? Are thoughts and feelings silent
In him who once has looked into the awful depths?
Thou art myself. Thou art no more than the negation
Of all it has been given me to feel and know.

To know? High time to know that in this world
Where'er one turns one finds but questions—never answers.
I who live and breathe do understand that in not-knowing
There is cause for lamentation only, not for fear.   (101)

The time has now come to combat despised reality and the
struggle for existence with reason and knowledge instead of
with art, or by identifying oneself with nature. It now seems
to Fet that only the mind, thought, pure knowledge, can raise
the individual above the crowd, give him power over the world
and emancipate him completely:

Bend tirelessly at your fated task
And the universe will reveal its blessings;
But think you not to be a god,

Nor, even in hours of inspiration,
With lifted eye and beaded brow,
Fear to face the bitter contrast,
Nor fail to say: This evil is, this good.

And if, upon the wings of pride
You dare, like a god, to know the skies,
Take not into the sacred realm
The bondsman's vain anxieties.

Circle aloft—all-powerful, all-seeing—
And from those vast unsullied heights
Evil and good, like cinerary ashes,
Will fall upon the crowd below.   (104)

Characteristically, the poet turns to man for the answer to all questions; but this time it is not man's ability to feel, sense, observe that he relies upon, but his ability to think.

In his earlier poems, Fet had reiterated one and the same idea: that he was part of nature, that he belonged to nature and that in his poems the voice of nature was heard. Now he feels that he speaks with the voice of the universe and quarrels with God, refusing to recognize His power to curb the individual's freedom. God, for Fet, represented the force determining the laws of nature on a cosmic scale, the force ruling over the universe, innocent of all ethical considerations.

In the poem cited above, "Dobro i zlo" ("Good and Evil"), Fet asserts that knowledge can elevate man to a realm that is holy and transform him into the likeness of a god, thereby releasing him from all ethical criteria. The following incident shows the difference between Fet's and Tolstoy's thinking: having received a letter containing Fet's "Alter Ego," Tolstoy and his wife objected to the simile in the couplet: "And I know that we were like gods when we gazed / At the stars in those other and happier days."

Fet replied to their objection:

As for the simile "like gods," . . . I know why it goes against the grain—you find a mythological allusion out of place here. But you know how hard it is to change any idea once accepted, especially in art. How would you express what I wanted to say with the words "like gods"—words as arrogant as demons with dilated nostrils, gloating not only in their power but in the exclusiveness of their power? "As if in paradise"?—flat and one-sided.[15]

For him, God and demon, even when treated with levity, were interchangeable concepts, since God was but the personification of unlimited power and eternal life without any moral attributes.

Fet contends that life, that is to say, the ability to change and develop, sets man above inanimate nature and establishes his affinity with the gods. Observing the heavens, Fet is struck by the difference between himself and the sun and reproaches God for not having given a mind to the great luminary, which is fated to obey the laws of life and even act as its source. The poet speaks of the sun contemptuously, as "a corpse with flaming visage." According to Fet, the existence and greatness of God is proven only by the inextinguishable flame, the inexhaustible energy, to be found in man. He addresses himself to God as if to prove the correctness of his view:

> Thou art omnipotent; defying comprehension
> Is the thought that I, a weak and fleeting creature,
> Should carry in my breast, like holiest seraphim,
> A light more fierce and bright than lights the universe;
>
> In me, who am the lowly prey of vanity,
> The plaything of her every whim and wile,
> This light, like Thee, is ever-present and eternal,
> Subjected not to tyrannies of time and space. (105)

The individual, an infinitesimal part of the universe, turns out to be equal to the whole of which he is a part—even greater than the whole. Thanks to the powers of mind, which can momentarily transfer the individual wherever he will, he is free while at the same time locked in space; he is mortal, yet partakes of immortality; and this union of incompatibles constitutes the miracle of the universe.

The longing to escape the confines of time and space is a constant theme of Fet's later lyrics. It results in his "break" with nature, and it determines the antireligious, irreconcilable character of his latest work. He utterly rejects the Christian concept of emancipation through the separation of soul and body at death. Fet is tireless in asserting that only life, physical life, the life of the body, confers divinity upon man. While vehemently denying that he is at the mercy of time, he insists that complete inner freedom depends on the oneness of soul and body, and their consumption in the impassioned flames of thought, love, and creative activity.

> All, all is mine, all that is and all that was;
> The bonds of time are not for dreams and fancies,
> Nor are divisions for the strivings of the soul,
> As if to say: here dreams of age, there dreams of youth!
>
> If only for a moment all is bright and joyous
> Beyond the bounds of the most crushing daily round.
> So long as in the body's crucible the soul
> Is captive, it can but follow where the wing doth lead;
>
> Speak not of happiness, nor yet of freedom,
> Where all is governed by the iron hand of fate.
> But here—here man no more is slave of nature,
> Nature herself is here a loyal slave.   (115)

In the poems of this period, the philosophical dream of escaping the bonds of time and space is persistently expressed in the imagery of flight. The sense of man's confinement in time and space, which, as we have noted, haunted Fet all his life (one of his first cycles, we recall, was entitled "The Passing Moment"), now becomes the tragic leitmotif of his philosophical lyrics.

The poet no longer finds "his native haunts" and "the home circle" a refuge. His affection for them has cooled. And this at a time when he has achieved the well-being he had so energetically sought, when he has made himself an ideal home, leaving one country house, which he had remodeled according to his taste, to build himself a much handsomer one.

Fet looked upon his sudden impulse to escape from the home circle experienced in the 1870's as "a temporary aberration." A poem of that time, the persona of which is a woman (Fet often resorted to this device), gives expression to a sudden irresistible desire for complete freedom, a desire to leave the hearth and home, the family, and dear, familiar places:

> All night the near ravine was noisy
> With rills and runnels coursing to the stream;
> In a final gush the 'wakened waters
> Sang the early triumph of the spring.
>
> You slept. I opened wide the casement.
> Cranes were crying in the steppe,
> And I was borne on wings of fancy
> Far beyond familiar places.
>
> Oh, to fly to trackless spaces,
> Past the woods and past the fields!
> And all the while the ground beneath me
> Trembled with the turbulence of spring. . . .   (141)

Here it is the lure of nature that makes the speaker long to fly away. At the call of spring, she is even ready to leave "her companion tried by troubles" to join the cranes in their flight. We detect a note often heard in Fet's earlier poetry—the affinity between man and all other living creatures.

Later, in the 1880's, it is not in order to merge with nature that the poet would leave the home circle, it is to soar proudly above nature in the realm of the spirit. He speaks of poetry, of poetry's indifference to suffering, and he contrasts immediate suffering, which animals feel, with the uplifting power of human beings to transform their immediate and personal feelings into "feeling-ideas" transcending egotistical values. Man is seen as the antithesis of the beast:

> Suffer! All things suffer. Even the dark beast suffers,
> All unknowing, all unsung.
> For him forever closed the door that leads
> To where suffering is tinged with joy.

It is easy to see that Fet's absorption in the world of ideas at this time was not a rejection of self-analysis, but rather a peculiar form of it. Addressing God, nirvana, death, he was first of all addressing his own instinctive fear of death, and doing so by posing a question that brought an emotional outburst in response. Between the lines we discover that the psychological aim of his philosophical verse was to expose and thus destroy his instinctive feelings: in other words, his philosophical lyrics assumed the function of psychoanalysis. This interpretation provides another argument supporting Fet's contention that poetry brings peace and resignation.

Now the poet sees his muse in cosmic space, withdrawn from the earth into the depths of the universe. She is:

> On a cloud, invisible to earth,
> In a crown of stars, an imperishable goddess
> Wearing a pensive smile upon her lips.   (301)

Again, let us not forget that the aspiration toward "worlds beyond the stars," toward the eternal and away from the fetters of earth and its relationships expressed by the hero of *Evening Lights* is nothing more than a tendency, not an inviolable rule.

Fet never solved for himself the problem of the relationship between real life, which, though finite, is alone capable of giving birth to eternal ideas, and the inanimate but infinite cosmos upon which all natural life depends (even the sun observes natural laws). His mind was concentrated with the same intensity upon the problem of emancipating man from the bonds of time and space.

In the poem "Never," the poet miraculously breaks through these barriers of time and space and, having done so, regrets it, for what he discovers is but the end of all life, the merging of earth and cosmos.

Returning to life after death, the poet finds himself in surroundings that are familiar but now leveled by snow, soundless and bereft of all life, human and animal. He sees the house he lived in, the park he strolled in; but without their accustomed setting in time and space they are no longer his house, his park, his village. They have lost meaning and function and have

thereby ceased to be man's home. The poet feels his oneness
with nature and all the creatures that once inhabited the earth:

> No winter birds, no gnats above the snow,
> I see it all: long since the earth has cooled
> And died: For whom is this hot breath
> Within me? For whom have I come back
> From the dark grave? With whom, with what,
> Is bound this consciousness? And to what end?
> Where shall I go, with no one to embrace
> In this vast wilderness where time is lost in space?   (106)

Consciousness loses its meaning when life is gone. The trans-
formation of time into eternity (into "Never") and the qualitative change in space make the earth uninhabitable for man.
The first condition of life—that eternal life for which all the
living so deeply yearn—is the continuation of the living environment, the existence in time and space of nature and human
beings. On returning to life from oblivion the hero of the poem
says to himself, "I must go home. How surprised they all will
be." As soon as he sees there is no one waiting for him, he
chooses to return to oblivion.

While rejecting immortality purchased at the price of the
living environment, Fet could not reconcile himself to the
thought of death as the inevitable companion of life. He was
possessed of a fierce love of life and its delights. In his reflective
poems he advanced the idea that philosophy, wisdom, knowledge,
and logic offer man a means of overcoming his fear of death
and, accordingly, death itself. But he himself saw and admitted
that this was only relatively satisfactory. What Strakhov called
his "pagan" love. of life could not be subdued by rational
argumentation. In his last years his most effective means of
achieving fullness of life and happiness was in the writing of
love lyrics.

A great many of the poems in *Evening Lights* are dedicated
to Mariya Lazich. Fet shows in them that his deathless, change-
less love for her and his quick sense of her presence despite the
passing of the years reduce to nothing the barriers of time and
death. In "Alter Ego," the theme of the conquest of time and
death is combined with the theme of the world of the spirit

where the poet and his love are supreme and where there are
no petty concerns of practical life or practical morality:

> As the lily bends over the mountain stream,
> So you did bend over the first of my songs;
> And whose was the triumph, if triumph there be?—
> The stream's or the lily's, the maid's or the song's?
>
> In the innocence of youth you understood all
> It was given me to say by mysterious powers;
> And while bitter my sentence of life without you,
> We are ever together; we cannot be parted.
>
> The grass that is greening on yonder far grave
> Grows greener with age in the crypt of my heart,
> And I know that we were as gods as we gazed
> At the stars in those other and happier days.
>
> Love has its words and these words cannot die.
> A particular judgment awaits you and me;
> We'll be quickly espied and plucked out of the crowd,
> And together we'll go; we cannot be parted.   (96)

The traditional use of green grass as a symbol of eternal life
is used here to indicate the freshness of the poet's memory of
her whom he loved. As long as that memory persists, so long
does his love, and with his love, his life.

In the last ten years of his life Fet wrote a new cycle of love
poems so uncharacteristic of anything he had written earlier,
so full of vitality, so erotically intense, presenting the image of
a woman so different from any encountered in his other lyrics,
that Bukhshtab justifiably reached the conclusion that they
must have been inspired by a true life experience unknown to
Fet's biographers.[16]

In these late love lyrics Fet does not speak of the home,
of the limited domestic circle presided over by women; rather,
he speaks of love and harmony as a flight into space and union
with the universe. These poems, replete with love's ecstasy,
are as much a revolt against nature's ruthless power as the
philosophical poems. It is not surprising that in the margin of
Alexander Blok's volume of Fet we see written again and again:

"He was 72 when he wrote this," "72 years old," "over 70." Fet seems to have written the poems to confound accepted opinions of what a man of his age represented. From all of them emanates the mood which found open declaration in the poem "Moego tot bezumstva zhelal" ("He Wanted My Madness"):

> Though age, the strumpet, would steal my last pleasure,
> My soul, e'er its setting, will come as before
> Direct to this spot like a bee to a blossom
> To feast on this fragrance and drink of this air.
>
> With happiness locked like a gem in my heart
> I will be a live echo of life's ebullition;
> This sweet-smelling honey is mine, is for me,
> For others the savorless wax of the comb.   (197)

In the attempt to break through the barriers confining the individual and limiting the possibilities of communicating with others, Fet wrote the poem "Now," as original in content as in title.

Addressing a young girl who will reach her maturity when Fet is no longer among the living, he foresees their future closeness achieved through his verse. He portrays himself speaking from out of the future to her as she will be in the future:

> With a maiden's thoughtful sensitivity
> You will understand the madness of my dreams,
> And all mean things on which I turned my back
> In quivering stanzas—and you will turn yours too.
>
> Put, then, your trust in greetings from the grave,
> In deathless love, the heart's elusive secrets,
> For from us both the air of timeless life is wafted
> And you and I will meet again—ah, now!   (110)

CHAPTER 6

Conclusion

TO what literary trend does Fet belong? Scholars differ in
their judgments. For a long time the opinion persisted in
Russian literary studies that he was a poet of the Romantic
school,[1] a poet forming a link between Zhukovsky's Romantic
lyrics of the beginning of the nineteenth century and the Symbolism of the end of the nineteenth century and the beginning
of the twentieth. In recent works of scholarship we find Fet's
name associated with Russian psychological Realism of the
nineteenth century.[2] Between these two extremes lie more
flexible opinions, such as Gustafson's, who . considers Fet a
Realist in depicting nature and a Romantic in his views on art.[3]

These differences in opinion spring from a serious study of
the processes determining the development of Russian poetry,
including the poetry of Fet, and each has sound arguments
behind it.

Russian literature developed with extraordinary intensity
during the nineteenth century, vehemently rejecting the old
and eagerly accepting the new. Fet, who lived long and wrote
poetry almost to the day of his death, witnessed various literary
periods. He was only twenty years younger than Pushkin; his
first collection of verse was published during Zhukovsky's lifetime; his last, when Anton Chekhov's talent was mature and
both Maksim Gorky and the Symbolists had appeared on the
literary scene. He remembered with what breathless anxiety
he had awaited Belinsky's criticism of his first book; his later
ones were reviewed by Strakhov and Solovev. His work was an
integral part of the great literary periods—the 1840's, the 1860's
and the 1880's—although he often found himself in bitter opposition to the prevailing style.

In the 1840's he appeared as a man nurtured upon the
Romantic poetry of the 1820's and 1830's, yet he immediately

146

found himself in the center of the literary and philosophical discussions agitating the best minds of the day. His response to these questions was original, and his poems of the 1840's were at once accepted as the voice of his generation. His poetry was loved by readers and praised by some critics, yet faulted by others for "morbidly" reflecting the conflict and confusion in the minds of the young people of that time.

In the 1860's, when the political struggle became most acute and a realignment of forces was occurring in society, Fet was told again and again that his poetry was out of date. His conflict with radical critics and democratically minded readers stimulated him to formulate his esthetic creed, which declared that art was and must be above passing considerations, especially problems of social progress.

Fet was, however, closely linked with the Realism of the middle of the century through his belief that the individual must always be at the center of the artist's attention, that man is the source of all beauty, and that it is he and his attempt to know himself and his environment (objective reality) that are the basic material with which the artist must work. As a matter of principle he excluded social and political themes from poetry, relegating man's political life to the sphere of "low" and prosaic activities. At the same time, his hero was an individual in tragic disharmony with his times. The historical and social struggle that Fet drove out of the door in his theoretical discussions came back in through the window of mood and intimation in his lyrics. Fet—and his contemporaries as well—could present the ideal anthropological man—natural and harmonious—and at the same time depict the conflict within the modern consciousness, even make a psychological analysis of the definite, concrete individual who was a product of those times and of that society.

Unquestionably, the esthetics of German philosophers, notably Schelling and Schopenhauer, influenced Fet's views on art, but, like other Russian Realistic writers, Fet saw their ideas through the prism of his own personality, and the original esthetic position he then assumed is best seen in his poetry rather than in his theoretical declarations.

For years Fet was in close contact with such outstanding

representatives of Russian Realistic literature as Tolstoy and Turgenev. They were the first readers of his verse; he solicited their advice and was guided by it. In return, he gave them his opinion of their finished works and suggested ideas for new ones. His advice was highly regarded.

Fet's influence upon the development of Russian Realistic literature is a fact, and not a mere supposition advanced by students of his work. Besides the spontaneity and keen powers of observation revealed in Fet's poetry, we have also seen its philosophical profundity. In the 1880's and 1890's, the imagery of his verse became richer, the meaning deeper. Young writers who in their revolt against Realism were venturing into the new field of Symbolism, sought features in Fet's philosophical poems that related them to Romantic poetry and lent the innovators assistance in working out their own style. Their re-examination of Fet was not limited to theoretical attempts to find a new interpretation of his poetry. Vladimir Solovev, one of the young poets close to the Symbolist movement, made Fet's acquaintance, wrote poems obviously influenced by the aging poet,[4] and himself sought to influence Fet's latest work by criticizing his poems and even proposing new versions of them.

It is, however, perfectly clear that the changes Fet's poetry underwent at this time were not sufficiently radical to ally him with the new literary movement. In his very last poetry he preserved organic ties with the poetry of the 1840's and 1860's. Without advancing beyond pure lyricism, he analyzed the development of psychological processes and described nature in growth and movement.

In the poetry of the 1880's and 1890's, Fet depicted nature as an objective phenomenon and thought as the product of human consciousness, dependent on man's psychological and, in the final analysis, physical state. Consequently, the reflective verse of the last ten years of his life assumed the form of monologues emanating from his own psychological state of mind and associated with his own particular world of emotions. In their eagerness to proclaim Fet the forerunner of Symbolism, theoreticians and writers of this movement were constrained to offer new readings and interpretations of his poetry.

By the end of the nineteenth century Fet had become one of the most popular poets in Russia. The peculiarity of his popularity lay in the fact that on the one hand he was hailed by young professionals of exclusive tastes who saw his work in a new light, and, on the other, his poetry had become part of the literary heritage of the broad masses, who did not always know its source.

The form of Fet's poetry, consisting exclusively of short, even very short, lyrics, made it not only easy to read but also easy to commit to memory. His longer poems, of which there are few and those second rate, never became popular, and the poet himself attached little significance to them. Toward the end of his life he declared he had no flair for the epic style.[5] The ease with which Fet's poems are memorized is based not only on their brevity but also on their exquisite finish, the subtle precision of intonation characteristic of his "conversational" verse, and the happy combination of euphony with the natural melodiousness of the Russian phrase in his "songs." Many of his lines have entered the Russian language as conversational clichés, greeted always by a smile of recognition. That fact accounts for the success of the numerous parodies of Fet's poetry. The story of its wide assimilation is inseparable from the history of Russian vocal music. On hearing familiar songs by Alexander Varlamov, Pyotr Bulakhov, Tchaikovsky, Nikolay Rimsky-Korsakov or Alexander Taneev played on the piano or the guitar, Fet's words inevitably come to mind, even though one may be unaware of their author.

Such popularity makes it difficult to distinguish what the poets of the following generation absorbed from him unconsciously, and what amounted to deliberate imitation or elaboration of his method.

It is easy to discover examples of the unconscious absorption of Fet's influence. Certainly, there was no conscious attempt to copy Fet when the peasant poet Ivan Surikov wrote "In the Shade of the Trees" in a manner reminiscent of Fet's "Distance." Surikov addresses his friend in the following words:

> Where are you now,
> My distant friend?

Sleeping in a flophouse?
Tramping the roads?
Pity your friend
So far away,
And in the silence of night
Remember me.[6]

The friend addressed is a peasant roaming the country in
search of employment and living by begging. Not only is the
structure of Surikov's poem borrowed, but the content, too,
echoes Fet's verse (the memory of an absent friend, the idea
of distance).

Another poet, a revolutionary, in writing about one of the
populists who "went to the people" to bring them enlightenment,
had so completely assimilated Fet's famous miniature "Whispers,"
that he instinctively used the form of the poem in describing
the poverty and suffering in the regions through which he
passed, a message as different as possible from that conveyed
by Fet's poem:

Fields, meadows,
Bright and clear expanses . . .
Deserted highroads . . .
Want in village huts . . .
Gendarmes in settlements,
Fines, taxes, tithes.[7]

These examples bear witness to the extent of the assimilation
and unconscious imitation of Fet's poetical forms, and also to
the impossibility of separating this unconscious assimilation
from the processes taking place in literature. In the volume of
his autobiography entitled *My Apprentice Days*, Gorky tells of
the artistic influences that aroused in him, a youth thrown into
society's "lower depths," a conscious aversion to "life's leaden
horrors" and nurtured aspirations toward the good and the
beautiful. In one episode from the book, Gorky relates how a
quotation from Fet spoken by a middle-aged intellectual enabled him, a workman's apprentice, to appreciate another's
suffering, and evoked in him admiration for the stranger's
intellectual world and appreciation of beauty: "Only the song
has need of beauty; / Beauty has no need of song."

"I was deeply impressed by these words and felt unaccountably sorry for the officer," wrote Gorky.

The chance overhearing of such words through an open window would scarcely make a lasting impression on an ordinary youth, but on Gorky, a workingman's apprentice, deprived as he was of the opportunity to pursue a systematic education and thirstily seizing upon every chance to "purify his soul" by "stripping it of impressions, as of fish scales, gathered from the bitter, poverty–stricken life" about him—for such a boy they were of enormous consequence. The young Gorky was ever in search of words that would assure him he was "not alone on this earth and would not become lost."[8] Fet's words were of that sort. That boy who heard them casually quoted by one of the poet's admirers himself became a writer, and moreover a fierce champion of a new and humane code of morality opposed to the cruel practices of his day. He accepted Fet's words in all their lyric spontaneity—not as a formal declaration, but as an outburst of exalted feeling inspired by the contemplation of the beautiful.

Vladimir Korolenko's novel *Mgnovenie* (*The Moment*) perhaps traces back to one of Fet's poems. It tells of the escape of a Spanish insurgent from imprisonment in a fort. He succeeds in filing through the bars of his window and crossing the bay in a boat. Fet recounts a similar story in his poem "Uznik" ("The Prisoner"), with which Korolenko must have been familiar. As usual, Fet depicts the "significant moment"; in this case, the moment when the prisoner is between bondage and freedom, the bonds almost severed but the flight not yet accomplished. This awareness gives rise to a fleeting sense of exaltation equal to the greatness of the moment.

It is the idea rather than the subject matter that makes Korolenko's story akin to Fet's poem, for that idea, as Korolenko himself defined it, is: "one instant of vital living is worth years of mere existing."[9]

Before the end of the nineteenth century Fet had no avowed followers among poets. To be sure, his kind of imagery, description, and observation is encountered now in one poet, now in another, but this fact does not demonstrate a conscious adoption of his artistic method by any of them. Indeed, his influence is felt more in prose than in poetry.

A great advance in the manner of describing nature was made by Russian prose writers in the second half of the nineteenth century. The great "landscape painters" in prose, Turgenev and Tolstoy, were unsurpassed. Like Fet, they revealed keen powers of observation and described nature in movement, and as seen through the prism of man's psychology. One can find much in common between the works of these two prose writers and Fet the poet, both in their general approach to nature and in the things they chose to depict. Obviously we are speaking here not of any "borrowing" from Fet, but of the similarity of their artistic approach.

When we come to Chekhov's landscapes, however, Fet's influence is patent. The writer Trigorin, from Chekhov's *The Seagull*, believed he was a born nature writer. "I love that water, the trees, the sky, I have a feeling for nature; she stirs me deeply and rouses in me an irresistible desire to write," he says. Another character from the play says of him, "Trigorin has worked out his devices. . . . On his canvas we see the glint of a broken bottle, the black shadow cast by a mill wheel and—there's a moonlit night for you!"[10]

This laconic method, by means of which a whole scene is suggested by a few well-chosen details acting upon the reader's sense of sight, sound, or smell, was introduced into Russian poetry by Fet. It was adapted to prose by Chekhov. Like Fet, Chekhov laid the greatest stress upon brevity, conciseness, economy of means. "I can speak shortly of long things," he once boasted. A special technique was required for the writing of his stories, whose rich content was conveyed as much by implication as by direct expression.

Like Fet, who compressed an entire landscape into a few lines of poetry by choosing the most vivid and significant details, Chekhov stimulated his readers' imagination and powers of observation, teaching them to draw their own conclusions. In *The Seagull*, Trigorin, a Realistic writer, is contrasted with Treplev, a seeker of new forms leading to Symbolism. Treplev selects his material from the sphere of abstract ideas and embodies them in symbols.

The artistic method of Fet as psychologist and Fet as landscape painter was congenial to Russian Realistic prose writers of the end of the nineteenth century. Chekhov was not alone in adopting Fet's manner of describing scenery. Many of his contemporaries, especially Ivan Bunin, did the same.

However, Fet's influence represents only one fine thread in the skein of literary traditions handed down to the twentieth century by the great Russian Realists of the nineteenth. The impulses generated by Fet's poetry and felt by the writers of later generations were not the most important and determinative; yet, although accepted more slowly and with greater difficulty by poetry than by prose, their influence on the former was more significant.

In the second half of the nineteenth century the development of Russian poetry was influenced mostly by Nekrasov. Social themes, lamentations over the suffering of the common folk by such "people's" poets as Pyotr Yakubovich, Surikov and Leonid Trefolev, lyrical "monologues of an intellectual killed by his 'troubled times'" by Simeon Nadson, stirred young people more deeply than Fet's reserved and refined lyrics concerned with universal subjects and requiring the reader to make the effort of reading between the lines in order fully to appreciate them. Some of Fet's poems were memorized, some were set to music and widely sung, yet when students gathered in the evening it was the poems of Nekrasov, Nadson, and Yakubovich that they recited and revolutionary songs by Pyotr Lavrov, Ivan Golts-Miller, Sergey Sinegub and Grigory Machtet that they sang. It was these poets, rather than Fet, who set the fashion in poetry in those days.

By the end of the century, Fet's influence increased owing to changes in the character of his own poetry, now dominated by philosophical themes, and also owing to the evolution of certain poets away from civil themes to philosophical subjects.

The philosopher and poet Vladimir Solovev, who declared himself a pupil and follower of Fet, transformed certain of Fet's esthetic pronouncements into universal canons. He looked upon all of the great poet's work as the embodiment of the sharp statements Fet had made in the heat of philosophical discussions. The widespread misconception that Fet was a poet who eschewed contemporaneity and addressed himself exclusively and immediately to eternity, can be traced back to Solovev's interpretation of him.

In 1890 Solovev wrote an article "On Lyric Poetry," in which he outlined his conception of Fet's verse. He based his conclusions on what he took to be a similar interpretation of spiritual processes by the mystics, on the one hand, and scientific materialists on the other. The revelation of the subconscious, the expression of an exalted love for woman having nothing in common with sexual attachment, sensitivity to the beauty of nature, and the creation of images conveying "a sense of the mysterious meaning both of human life and of the life of nature"[11]—these, according to Solovev, formed the basic content of Fet's poetry. Such an interpretation tore the poet's roots from the living soil, glossed over his gifts as a psychologist and observer of nature, turned his imagery into the symbolic reflection of "eternal verities," and transformed the love he felt for a flesh-and-blood woman and the tragedy of losing her (to which no philosophy could reconcile him) into the poetic adoration of abstract Woman.

Such a conception of Fet's poetry was also congenial to the Symbolists, who "progressed from immediate images, beautiful in themselves, to the abstract ideal concealed within them."[12] They accepted Fet as one of the precursors of their artistic style, reading symbols into his philosophical and love lyrics to bring them into line with their theories.

Fet's philosophical poems lent themselves more easily to such a reading than did his love and nature lyrics. The very abstract nature of Fet's latest poems; the significant use therein of logical concepts often expressed in exalted terms; the abundance of hyperbolic, cosmic imagery as well as of imagery embodying abstract ideas; the recurrence of word-images emotionally and semantically constant in poetry (death, God, nothingness, heaven, stars, sunrise)—these elements established a kinship with the late nineteenth-century poets who, for the development of their own method, had only to renounce the lyrical concreteness of his verse and substitute symbolic matter for its psychological implications.

Even the title of Fet's last books, *Evening Lights,* might be understood as symbolic of the withdrawal of his muse and of the eternal light of poetry. This title expressed the principal image; it resembled the imagery of the individual poems in the collections and united them biographically, thematically, and emotionally into what might be accepted as one great cycle.

Collections of poetry with symbolic titles suggesting the themes and the principle uniting the poems were popular at the end of the nineteenth century and the beginning of the twentieth. *Evening Lights* reveals something about the author—that he is a man in the evening of life—and about the place of these poems in his life—that they are late works. Autobiographical considerations lay at the basis of collections published by Andrey Bely and Valery Bryusov, and their books, too, were given symbolic titles. In a note, "In Lieu of a Preface" introducing *Urna* (*The Urn*), Andrey Bely explains the relationship between the titles of his collections *Zoloto v lazuri* (*Gold in the Azure*), *Pepel* (*Ashes*), and *Urna* (*The Urn*)—and the philosophical stage of his development they reflect. Bryusov's cycles of poetry similarly mirror the periods of intellectual development through which he passed.[13]

Fet's influence can be sensed in Alexander Blok's early cycle of poems "Stikhi o Prekrasnoi dame" ("About the Lady Beautiful"). While noting this influence, critics point out the fundamental changes wrought in Fet's themes and imagery by Blok's "divesting them of their concrete associations and conferring upon them purely symbolic significance." The poems of the young Blok, unlike Fet's poems, are purely figurative. In his "Lady Beautiful" poems, Blok develops those enduring word-symbols used throughout his entire work and in every new poem.[14] These words, divorced from their original meaning, become bearers of a new significance.

Working along this line, Blok later reinterpreted Fet's "Za gran'iu proshlykh let" ("Over the Border of the Past"), using these words as the title of one of his late books. He acknowledges having borrowed them from Fet, asserting that they had become "his lodestar."

Fet's influence upon Blok is too deep and complex a question to be dismissed simply by citing instances of conscious borrowing or of unconscious duplication. Blok studied Fet carefully.

The complete edition of Fet's works owned by Blok is full of notes and comments in his hand. In this edition we find checks beside certain poems in the index; about a dozen code signs in the text denoting Blok's response; the underscoring of what Blok felt to be particularly happy or unhappy expressions; and marginal comments on the work of Boris Nikolsky, the editor of this edition. For example, in the foreword to Volume I, Nikolsky writes: "The overwhelming majority of his poems are not only unconnected with social events or even with events in his own life; they might have been written in any country and at any time"—to which Blok exclaims in the margin, "Oh, no!"

Nikolsky's arbitrary grouping of certain of Fet's poems under the title of "The Heart" aroused Blok's indignation, for no such cycle of poems had existed in Fet's lifetime.

Blok organized his own poems into cycles and assigned great importance to the central image that gave unity to each cycle. In some cases, these images were strikingly like Fet's, as for instance, his "The Snow Mask," suggesting Fet's "Snow," and "Nightingale Garden," suggesting Fet's "The Nightingale and the Rose." Blok adopted many of Fet's images, giving them exalted, often mystical, significance. Images from Fet's "Solovei i roza" ("The Nightingale and the Rose") and the expression "the joy of suffering," from "My Muse" (1887), were accorded symbolic meaning in Blok's drama *The Rose and the Cross*. Blok underlined the expression ". . . sweet-scented sphere" from the poem "Zavtra—ia ne razlichaiu" ("Tomorrow—I see No Difference,") and ". . . sweet-smelling sphere" from "Pochemu?" ("Why?"). He was impressed by Fet's recurrent use of the image of a ring, a circle, a sphere, and used it in his own poems in much the same way, namely, to indicate. a woman's sphere of influence, her "magnetic field":

> She appeared. Now eclipsed were
> All the fair ones, all her friends,
> And my heart I knew had entered
> The enchanted circle she defined.[15]

Blok, however, did not attach primary importance to the immediate significance of the image as a circle into which one is drawn by the power of another: for him, its chief meaning lay in the chain of associations evoked by the symbolic, even mystical, significance of a circle.

Despite the great difference between the poetic approaches of Blok and Fet[16] it should be noted that Blok, who was more "psychological" than any of the other Russian Symbolists, and who had thoroughly mastered the traditions of Russian Critical Realism of the nineteenth century, had assimilated Fet's poetry more thoroughly than his contemporaries, and comprehended the older poet's achievements more profoundly. He was interested not only in Fet's philosophical lyrics. He shared with Fet the ability to perceive scarcely perceptible signs of the "flow" of life in nature and at the same time to capture the general tone of a particular landscape. To his successors, Fet revealed possibilities of expanding associations and of complicating psychological relationships by the use of implication. By following and elaborating upon this method, Blok vastly extended its potential and thus enriched the idiom of poetry.

Blok loved the concreteness and vitality of Fet's poetic allusions and recognized their importance for the further development of poetry. He underlined the third and fourth lines of the first quatrain of "U kamina" ("At the Fireplace"), and wrote in the margin: "Andrey Bely traces back to this."

> The firelight is dying. In twilight dusk
> The flames translucent flutter,
> As flutters the turquoise wing of a moth
> Round the scarlet heart of a poppy. (274)

Blok was also keenly sensitive to the psychological portraits of the Russian Hamlet and Ophelia created by Fet. The Hamlet of his own making reflects the persona's sense of his tragic ties with history. Blok appreciated Fet's melancholy, revealing the deep tragedy of a stagnant life:

> Stop your grumbling, my purrsome pussy,
> As you motionless lie, half asleep,
> It is dreary enough without your complaint—
> Dreary and cold and dark.

With you not here the stove still stands as it stood,
The window still gapes as it gaped,
And the door and the candle and everything else—
And the same old despair.... (249–50)

If Fet depicts in this poem the dismal routine of one dull
day following another (time which is no time), Blok was
filled with the horror of one dull year following another, the
troubled years:

> Night, street, lamppost, drugstore,
> Dim and meaningless light.
> Given another twenty-five winters,
> Nothing will change. No escape.
> You die. The cycle begins all over,
> Goes on in the same old groove:
> Night. The rippling chill of the river,
> Lamppost, drugstore, street.[17]

In Blok's poem, as in Fet's, the cataloguing of objects typical
of the scene creates an image of the eternal, the world "beyond
time" surrounding man. In painting such a picture, neither of
the poets denied the existence of time, as Fet was sometimes
said to do; rather, they expressed their morbid sense of the
stoppage of time, and the nightmare this represented for them.
Unlike Fet, Blok accepted time as a historical category. Immobility was for him not merely an image of death, but of a
"freezing" of society similar to death, though it be but for a
time. In his poem *Vozmezdie* (*Vengeance*) the period of reaction in the 1880's is seen as a period when the country was
hypnotized into troubled, enforced sleep.

Blok's world was not frozen in time and space. It was swept
by the winds of history. Blok was always true to his own artistic method, his own poetic idiom, the course he himself had
chosen in literature, and the many quotations from Fet we
find in his verse are not the sum of Fet's influence upon Blok.
Fet was not Blok's teacher, and his poetry was not the source
from which the younger genius sprang, but Fet was still one of
Blok's favorite poets, and it with with Blok that the serious and
detailed study of Fet's contribution to Russian poetry began.

Blok appreciated the music of Fet's poetry. He made use of the stanza structure Fet introduced and of his favorite meters. Konstantin Balmont, Blok's contemporary, elaborated upon Fet's use of sound in poetry, making sound one of the main devices for creating the image, but Balmont understood the use of sound as the invention of a series of sounds evoking associations (sound imitation) and the discovery of euphonious combinations, while for Blok, as for Fet, the use of sound was a more abstract and philosophical problem, serving the high purposes of art, and rendering a special service in putting an end to man's sense of isolation.

Vladimir Mayakovsky, the poet-orator, was in every respect the direct antithesis of Fet. An urban writer by conviction, he threw down the gauntlet to his brother poets:

> While they are mixing, to the sawing of rhymes,
> A brew of roses and nightingales,
> The street is writhing without a tongue,
> It cannot cry out, it cannot even talk.[18]

In asserting that "the god of the city is tramping over plowed fields, flaying the word," he made it clear that the day for poetry describing quiet, rural scenes, fenced-in patriarchal homes, and the harmonious merging of man and nature, was over. He believed that the times demanded other imagery and other sounds than the wonderfully harmonious sounds of Fet's poetry. The new poetry should be set to drums rather than the flute. He declared that Fet's imagery was "pretty" and over-refined, and that the music of his verse was produced by an artificial selection of sounds. These charges came naturally from one whose world of poetry was so different from Fet's. And yet Mayakovsky admitted that when he was alone in his study he sometimes immersed himself in the verse of Fet, Tyutchev, and Innokenty Annensky.[19] In other words, Fet was one of Mayakovsky's antecedents, too, but one against whom he took up the cudgels. Yet, once when selecting five names representing Russian poetry, Mayakóvsky chose Mikhail Lomonosov, Pushkin, Tyutchev, Fet and Nekrasov.[20]

What Mayakovsky found archaic and doomed to extinction in Fet's poetry other poets of Mayakovsky's generation found congenial, and they continued the trend notwithstanding the enormous popularity of Mayakovsky, who introduced a new epoch in poetry.

Sergey Esenin, a poet who sang of the village and country-side and was tragically unable to accept urban life, adapted himself in his own way to Fet's tradition. Like Fet, he built up the image of his native land through scenes of his own home and village. There was, however, a sharp social difference between the picture presented by Esenin, a poet of peasant origin, and Fet the wealthy landowner. This difference is expressed lexically and intonationally, Esenin holding closer to the folklore tradition. The two poets are akin, nonetheless, in their love of the mellow beauty of their native land, their ability to see this beauty in the daily life about them, and their manner of expressing themselves simply and spontaneously. There are instances when Esenin borrows directly from Fet. His "Birch," for instance, is only a variation on the theme of Fet's "Sad Is the Birch Beside My Window."

It is a curious coincidence that both Fet and Esenin make oriental verse the background of poems about the Russian village and countryside, and contrast the passions of the strong, undivided oriental character with the love of "sons of the North" (Fet's "In Imitation of Oriental Poetry" and Esenin's "Persian Themes").

In some respects the poetry of Anna Akhmatova is reminiscent of Fet's. Strangely enough, Fet often let a woman speak in the first person in his poems. Later, Blok used the same device. Fet's remarkable understanding of a woman's emotional nature must have appealed to female poets, who found in his verse an original interpretation of the feminine lyrical individuality.

Fet's attitude to his literary calling anticipated Akhmatova's in many ways. Both brought a high level of literary culture to their labor; both were completely immersed in the world of art; both demanded simplicity, truthfulness, and stern candor in the expression of their emotions, a meticulous selection of artistic means, and the achievement of the greatest possible conciseness. Fet's description of his muse as "bathed in the air of simplicity" could be as aptly applied to Akhmatova's. Both poets were imbued with a sense of the lofty and lasting

significance of poetry. The affinity between them is made clear
by comparing Fet's "To My Muse" (1882) with Akhmatova's
"My Muse." The imagery of the two poems is similar. For both
Fet and Akhmatova, the muse was as simple and modest as a
shepherdess, yet ruling over a world of stern majesty and de-
manding self-abnegation and self-sacrifice in her service. Both
poems begin with a visit from the modest guest and end in a
hymn to her greatness. Fet's poem opens with the words:

> You came and sat beside me. Happy and disturbed,
> I murmured softly your caressing stanzas;
> And though you may despise my gifts,
> No quarrel can you pick with my devotion. . . .   (301)

Akhmatova's:

> When in the night I await her coming,
> My very life seems hanging by a thread.
> And what to me is honor, youth, or freedom,
> When this sweet maid appears with pipe in hand?
> Ah, she has come. Pulling off my blanket,
> She looks at me with an attentive eye.
> "Was it you," I, ask, "who did dictate to Dante
> His purgatory pages?" "It was I," is her reply.[21]

Anna Akhmatova belonged to that group of poets at the beginning of the twentieth century who wished to reinstate the
world of real objects and plastic forms after their rejection by
the Symbolists in favor of abstractions, of the "essence," rather
than its objective image. She deliberately took up and further
developed the traditions of classical verse. Her delicate miniatures describing the beauties of the lakes and oak woods of
Tsarskoe Selo, or giving expression to moments of poetic meditation, or recounting the loveliness of antique statues, undoubtedly reflect Pushkin's influence, but Akhmatova did not ignore
Fet's achievements in the anthological form. Her poem "Tsar-
skosel'skaia statuia" ("A Statue in Tsarskoe Selo"), was
written in response to Pushkin's classical quatrain of the same
name and was inspired by the same statue; indeed, Akhmatova
addresses Pushkin in her poem. And yet the structure of the

verse owes more to Fet's "Diana" than to Pushkin's poem. She draws a picture of the statue at the edge of a pool surrounded by trees, and voices the "vague fear" inspired in her by the contemplation of the maiden's "eternal youth," the deathless-ness denied the living. The last lines of the poem: "Look, she rejoices in her sorrow, / So elegant in her nudity"[22] have little in common with Pushkin's style, but might almost have been written by Fet, expressing as they do a penchant for paradox characteristic of him ("rejoices in her sorrow"; "so elegant in her nudity").

Akhmatova wrote two poems called "On Reading Hamlet," in which she presents an Ophelia strong in character, as op-posed to Hamlet, and one who appropriates his aphorisms. This Ophelia is a far cry from Fet's, and we have no grounds for accusing Akhmatova of imitating the older poet, but the very fact of her having treated the same theme demonstrates the continuity of the tradition descending through Fet to Akhmatova.

The image of the willow tree, symbol of femininity and of Fet's sad Northern homeland, as expressed in his poem "To Ophelia," became one of Akhmatova's favorite images. She jux-taposed the confusion and conflict of her inner world with the beauty and harmony of Pushkin's ideal man, and this juxtaposi-tion, counteracting the subjectivity and pain of her emotions, conferred upon them a stern, poetic loftiness.

Akhmatova's mastery in expressing complicated emotions in simple and modest terms, as well as her command of slight forms whose themes are enriched by implication and association, made her a true follower of Fet. She was, however, much more than a follower: she was an original poet in her own right, who was able to cull what her talent required from the rich store left by this representative of nineteenth-century poetry.

Fet's influence on contemporary Soviet literature can be seen in the work of such nature poets as Nikolay Zabolotsky and Boris Pasternak, and even in that of more youthful writers.

Fet continues to live in literature. His poems are read; he teaches others to see the world around them and to love it— to love it because it is life itself. The new poets commune with Fet and often argue with him fiercely as they formulate their own artistic credos.

Notes and References

Preface

1. V. G. Belinskii, *Polnoe sobranie sochinenii* (Moscow, 1956), XII, 124. Cited below as: Belinsky.
2. A. Grigor'ev, *Sochineniia* (St. Petersburg, 1876), I, 85. Cited below as: Grigorev.

Chapter One

1. A. A. Fet, *Rannie gody moei zhizni* (Moscow, 1893), p. 141. This fact is also mentioned in a letter of May 23, 1888, from Fet to Yakov Polonsky. On this see G. Blok, *Rozhdenie poeta* (Trudy Pushkinskogo doma pri Rossiiskoi Akademii nauk) (Leningrad, 1924), p. 100. Cited below as: Blok, *Rozhdenie poeta.*
2. A. A. Fet, *Polnoe sobranie stikhotvorenii* (2nd ed., Leningrad, 1959), p. 381. Page references to Fet's poetry included in the text will be to this edition.
3. Fet, *Rannie gody moei zhizni*, p. 54.
4. *Ibid.*, pp. 105–10.
5. Richard F. Gustafson, *The Imagination of Spring: The Poetry of Afanasy Fet* (New Haven and London, 1966), pp. 42–45. Cited below as: Gustafson.
6. A. S. Pushkin, *Polnoe sobranie sochinenii* (Moscow-Leningrad, 1949), III, 471. Cited below as: Pushkin.
7. Gustafson, pp. 84–98.
8. Blok, *Rozhdenie poeta*, p. 61.
9. *Biblioteka dlia chteniia*, No. 1, 1841, section VI, 1, 3.
10. *Otechestvennye zapiski*, No. 12, 1840, 42.
11. Belinsky, XI, 584.
12. Fet, *Rannie gody moei zhizni*, pp. 152–153.
13. A. Grigor'ev, *Vospominaniia* (Moscow-Leningrad, 1930), p. 190.
14. Grigorev, I, 86–96.
15. Fet, *Rannie gody moei zhizni*, p. 209.
16. Letter of April 7, 1887, from Fet to K. R. (Konstantin Romanov), preserved in the archive of the Institute of Russian Litera-

ture of the USSR Academy of Sciences. The letter is quoted by
P. P. Gromov in his introductory article to A. A. Fet, *Stikhotvoreniia*
(Moscow-Leningrad, 1963), p. 35. The same notion was also expressed in Fet's article "O stikhotvoreniiakh F. Tiutcheva," *Russkoe
slovo*, February 1859, section "Kritika," p. 80.

Chapter Two

1. See the article by B. Ia. Bukhshtab in A. Fet, *Polnoe sobranie
stikhotvorenii* (Leningrad, 1959), pp. 8–9. Cited below as: Bukhshtab.

2. Fet, *Rannie gody moei zhizni*, p. 258.

3. *Otechestvennye zapiski*, No. 1, 1850, p. 71.

4. Grigorev, I, 85.

5. Bukhshtab, p. 62.

6. Gustafson, pp. 140–42.

7. A. I. Herzen, *Sobranie sochinenii v 30-kh tomakh* (Moscow,
1956), VII, 208, 222–23. Cited below as: Herzen.

8. M. Iu. Lermontov, *Polnoe sobranie sochinenii* (Moscow-Leningrad, 1948), I, 72.

9. N. V. Gogol', *Polnoe sobranie sochinenii* (Leningrad, 1951),
VI, 220. Cited below as: Gogol.

10. Iu. M. Lotman, "Problema khudozhestvennogo prostranstva v
proze Gogolia," *Trudy po russkoi i slavianskoi filologii*, XI, vyp. 209.
Tartuskii gosudarstvennyi universitet, Tartu, 1968, p. 49.

11. The characterization of isolated country life as existence with
a "ringlike topography" was used by Gogol in his famous story
"Starosvetskie pomeshchiki." See Iu. M. Lotman, *op. cit.*, pp. 22–23.
This correspondence in descriptive method between Gogol and Fet
would seem significant. For Fet, like Gogol, describes the patriarchal
village in an idealized and poetic way, while simultaneously remark-
ing that this magnificent "refuge" is quite melancholy.

12. Pushkin, III, 126.

13. *Ibid.*, V, 103.

14. This poem, like many others from the 1850 collection, underwent reworking by Fet for the 1856 edition at the request of the
editor, Turgenev. The final quatrain was deleted.

15. Fet, *Polnoe sobranie stikhotvorenii*, pp. 170, 694. In both the
first (1937) and second editions of Fet's collected verse is printed
the latest version of the ending of this poem, with the initial version
given in the "Early Redactions" section.

16. Grigorev, I, 95, 82.

17. *Ibid.*, pp. 96, 99.

18. F. I. Tiutchev, *Polnoe sobranie stikhotvorenii* (Moscow-Leningrad, 1939), pp. 49–50. Cited below as: Tyutchev.

19. Bukhshtab has provided a subtle and convincing reading of this poem. He has demonstrated the complex structure of a poem which is calculated to initiate the reader into a series of branch associations on the author's part. Without an understanding of them, the work seems "mysterious and incomprehensible." Bukhshtab, pp. 38–39.

20. I. S. Turgenev, *Polnoe sobranie sochinenii i pisem* (Moscow-Leningrad, 1962), *Pis'ma*, IV, 330. Cited below as: Turgenev.

21. Pushkin, III, 127.

22. Tyutchev, p. 125.

23. Gustafson, pp. 171–73; B. Eikhenbaum, *Melodika russkogo liricheskogo stikha* (Petrograd, 1922), pp. 156–57. Cf. K. I. Chukovskii, *Iskusstvo perevoda* (Moscow-Leningrad, 1936), pp. 62–63; and Oleksandr Finkel', *Teoriia i praktika perekladu* (Kharkov, 1929), pp. 150–51.

24. Letter of December 27, 1886, to K. R. See the collection *Russkie pisateli o literature,* Vol. I (Leningrad, 1939), 447.

25. Pushkin, IV, 239.

26. V. G. Korolenko, *Sobranie sochinenii* (Moscow, 1956), X, 219. Cited below as: Korolenko.

27. It is noteworthy that V. M. Zhirmunsky has detected a linkage between another poem of Fet's, "Ia polon dum, kogda zakryvshi vezhdy," with this same poem of Goethe's. Boris Eikhenbaum, in agreement with this thesis, has done an interesting comparison of the compositions of these two poems of Goethe and Fet: B. M. Eikhenbaum, *Melodika russkogo liricheskogo stikha,* pp. 148–49. See also Eikhenbaum's *O poezii* (Leningrad, 1969), p. 464. The 1969 edition is cited below as: Eikhenbaum, *Melodika.*

28. *Russkoe slovo,* February 1859, section "Kritika," p. 72.

29. *Russkii vestnik,* No. 11 (1881), pp. 233–38.

Chapter Three

1. Letter of June 5, 1853, from Ivan Turgenev to Sergey Aksakov: Turgenev, *Pis'ma,* II, 165.

2. Gogol, VIII, 50.

3. *Ibid.,* 55.

4. Belinsky, V, 257.

5. N. A. Nekrasov, *Polnoe sobranie sochinenii* (Moscow, 1950), IX, 205. Cited below as: Nekrasov.

6. Turgenev, *Pis'ma,* VIII, 118.

7. *Ibid.*, II, 268–69.

8. After Fet's death, a copy of the 1850 edition of Fet's verse, recording the initial efforts of Turgenev and Fet in preparing the 1856 edition, was found in his library. It used to belong to a relative of the poet's wife, I. S. Ostroukhov, and therefore is now called the "Ostroukhov copy." This copy is now preserved in the archive of the Tretyakov State Art Galley in Moscow.

9. Fet, *Moi vospominaniia*, I, 104–105.

10. Iu. A. Nikol'skii, "Materialy po Fetu. I. Ispravleniia Turgenevym fetovskikh *Stikhotvorenii* 1850 goda," *Russkaia mysl'*, vol. 8–9 (1921), 211–27; vol. 10–12, 248–62; D. D. Blagoi, "Turgenev–redaktor Feta," *Pechat' i revoliutsiia*, Vol. 3 (1923), 45–64; N. Kolpakova, "Iz istorii fetovskogo teksta," *Poetika*, No. 3 (Vremennik slovesnogo otdela Instituta istorii iskusstv) (Leningrad, 1927), pp. 168–87.

11. B. Ia. Bukhshtab, "Sud'ba literaturnogo nasledstva A. A. Feta. Obzor," *Literaturnoe nasledstvo*, No. 22–24 (Moscow, 1935), p. 568.

12. Turgenev, *Pis'ma*, II, 334.

13. Bukhshtab, "Sud'ba literaturnogo nasledstva Feta," p. 567.

14. Pushkin, III, 59.

15. Nekrasov, IX, 336.

16. V. P. Botkin, *Sochineniia* (St. Petersburg, 1891), II, 381. Cited below as: Botkin.

17. F. M. Dostoevskii, *Polnoe sobranie sochinenii* (St. Petersburg, 1895), IX, 79.

18. Bukhshtab, p. 56.

19. *Moskvitianin*, No. 21 (1854), p. 41.

20. Fet, *Moi vospominaniia*, I, 59.

21. Gromov, "A. A. Fet," p. 46.

22. Gustafson, pp. 165–214.

23. *Ibid.*, pp. 175, 178.

24. Grigorev, I, 86–96.

Chapter Four

1. Botkin, II, 368.

2. M. E. Saltykov-Shchedrin, *Polnoe sobranie sochinenii* (Moscow, 1937), V, 330.

3. Fet, *Polnoe sobranie stikhotvorenii* (St. Petersburg, 1901), II, 487, 489.

4. Herzen, VI, 326.

5. Gogol, VIII, 472.

6. *Literaturnoe nasledstvo*, No. 37–38 (Moscow, 1939), p. 210.

7. Bukhshtab, p. 55.

8. L. N. Tolstoi, *Perepiska s russkimi pisateliami* (Moscow, 1962), p. 257.

9. *Ibid.*, p. 246.

10. *Russkoe slovo*, No. 2 (1859), pp. 64, 65.

11. See B. Ia. Bukhshtab, "Esteticheskie vzgliady Feta," *Literaturnaia ucheba*, No. 12 (1936), p. 39; Bukhshtab, "Fet," pp. 57–59; and Gustafson, pp. 25–26.

12. *Russkoe slovo*, No. 2 (1859), pp. 68, 69.

13. The question of Schopenhauer's influence on Fet is discussed in the above mentioned works by Bukhshtab (*Literaturnaia ucheba*, pp. 39–41; "Fet," pp. 19–22, 66–67); in P. P. Gromov's "A. A. Fet," in Fet, *Stikhotvoreniia* (3rd ed., 1963), pp. 68–72; and in Gustafson, pp. 14–28.

14. Pushkin, II, 274.

15. Analyses of numerous poems by Fet from the viewpoint of their melodic structure, as well as analyses of the melodic organization of Fet's works as a whole may be found in Eikhenbaum's *Melodika*, pp. 435–509. For an analysis of the sound structure of some poems which Eikhenbaum did not treat, see Bukhshtab, pp. 44–50.

16. For an analysis of Fet's verses on music, see Eikhenbaum's *Melodika*, pp. 485–89 and 491–94; Bukhshtab, p. 71; and Gustafson, pp. 189–205.

17. M. Chaikovskii, *Zhizn' Petra Il'icha Chaikovskogo* (Moscow and Leipzig, 1902), III, 266–67.

18. Eikhenbaum maintains that in Fet's poetry the element of the song and romance predominates over the rhythmic and the plastic. See his *Melodika*, pp. 446–47.

Chapter Five

1. A. A. Fet, *Stikhotvoreniia* (Moscow, 1863), I, 1.

2. *Ibid.*, II, 6.

3. Bukhshtab, pp. 25–26.

4. Fet, *op. cit.*, II, 66.

5. His translations from Hafiz were made from the translations by G. Daumer, *Hafis. Eine Sammlung persischer Gedichte* (Hamburg, 1856). Fet borrowed a few phrases from Daumer's foreword to this edition for his article on Hafiz. Since, like many of his contemporaries, Fet had a high opinion of the ability of German translators, he was convinced that Daumer's translations were quite precise. In fact, however, Daumer's "translations" from Hafiz were

nothing more than poetic stylizations. See Fet, *Polnoe sobranie stikhotvorenii* (Moscow, 1959), pp. 826–27.

6. Turgenev, *Pis'ma*, VIII, 285.

7. I. S. Turgenev, *Polnoe sobranie sochinenii i pisem. Sochineniia* (Moscow-Leningrad, 1967), XIV, 36.

8. See the note in Fet, *Polnoe sobranie stikhotvorenii* (Moscow, 1959), p. 716.

9. Turgenev, *Pis'ma*, VI, 99.

10. L. N. Tolstoi, *Polnoe sobranie sochinenii* (Moscow, 1953), LXII, 294, 303.

11. See Bukhshtab, pp. 66–68.

12. The comparing of death with a "calf's-foot jelly" is Fet's ironic way of referring to the image from Turgenev's short story "Prizraki" ("Phantoms"), where death is portrayed as a living, moving and predatory cloud. The door to nothingness is an image found in Prince Andrey's dying dream in Tolstoy's novel *War and Peace*.

13. Tolstoy, *Perepiska s russkimi pisateliami*, pp. 295–97.

14. *Ibid.*, p. 297.

15. *Ibid.*, pp. 354–55.

16. Bukhshtab, p. 65.

Chapter Six

1. I. G. Iampol'skii, "Poeziia shestidesiatykh godov (obshchii obzor)," *Istoriia russkoi literatury* (Moscow-Leningrad, 1956), VIII, 17–22; L. Ginzburg, *O lirike* (Moscow-Leningrad, 1964), pp. 250–83.

2. Bukhshtab, pp. 77–78; Gromov, "A. A. Fet," pp. 45–49; L. M. Lotman, "Liricheskaia i istoricheskaia poeziia 50–70-kh godov," *Istoriia russkoi poezii* (Leningrad, 1969), II, 136–37.

3. Gustafson, p. 15.

4. P. Gromov, *Geroi i vremia* (Leningrad, 1961), p. 404.

5. Fet, *Moi vospominaniia*, I, 7.

6. *I. Z. Surikov i poety-surikovtsy* (Moscow-Leningrad, 1966), p. 113.

7. *Vol'naia russkaia poeziia vtoroi poloviny XIX veka* (Leningrad, 1959), p. 358.

8. M. Gor'kii, *Sobranie sochinenii* (Moscow, 1951), XIII, 352, 357–58.

9. Korolenko, II, 398.

10. A. P. Chekhov, *Sochineniia* (Moscow, 1948), II, 167, 189.

11. V. S. Solov'ev, *Sobranie sochinenii* (St. Petersburg, 1901), VI, 235.

12. K. D. Bal'mont, *Gornye vershiny* (Moscow, 1904), I, 94.

13. See L. Ginzburg, *O lirike* (Moscow-Leningrad, 1964), p. 272.

14. *Ibid.*, pp. 280–83.

15. A. Blok, *Sobranie sochinenii* (Moscow-Leningrad, 1960), II, 254. Cited below as: Blok.

16. See P. Gromov, *Blok, ego predshestvenniki i sovremenniki* (Leningrad, 1966), pp. 18–31.

17. Blok, III, 37.

18. V. Maiakovskii, *Polnoe sobranie sochinenii* (Moscow, 1955), I, 181.

19. *Ibid.*, I, 112.

20. *Ibid.*, XII, 388.

21. A. Akhmatova, *Beg vremeni* (Moscow-Leningrad, 1965), p. 254.

22. *Ibid.*, p. 124.

Selected Bibliography

PRIMARY SOURCES

In Russian:

Polnoe sobranie stikhotvorenii. Ed. B. Ia. Bukhshtab. Leningrad: Sovetskii pisatel' (Biblioteka poeta, Bol'shaia seriia), 1936.
Polnoe sobranie stikhotvorenii. Ed. B. Ia. Bukhshtab. Second edition, Leningrad: Sovetskii pisatel' (Biblioteka poeta, Bol'shaia seriia), 1959.
Stikhotvoreniia. Ed. B. Ia. Bukhshtab. Leningrad, 1956.
"O stikhotvoreniiakh F. Tiutcheva," *Russkoe slovo,* No. 2 (1859), section "Kritika," pp. 63–84.
Russkie pisateli o literature (XVII–XX vv.). Leningrad, 1939, I, 432–55.
Moi vospominaniia (1848–1889). 2 vols. Moscow, 1890.
Rannie gody moei zhizni. Moscow, 1893.

In English:
Bowring, J. et al. *A Second Book of Russian Verse.* London: Macmillan, 1948.
Coxwell, Charles. *Russian Poems.* London: Macmillan, 1929.
Eastman, Max et al. *A Treasury of Russian Verse.* New York: Macmillan, 1949.
Wiener, Leo. *Anthology of Russian Literature.* New York: Putnam, 1903, vol. II.

SECONDARY SOURCES

Note: Annotations for secondary sources were supplied by the editor.

Bal'mont, K. D. *Gornye vershiny.* Moscow: Grif, 1904, I, 63–71, 89–92. A comparison of Pushkin and Lermontov, who live within time, with Tyutchev and Fet, who live within eternity; followed by a contrast between Tyutchev and Fet.
Blok, G. *Rozhdenie poeta: Povest' o molodosti Feta.* Leningrad: Vremia, 1924. A biographical novel about Fet's youth.
Botkin, V. P. "Stikhotvoreniia A. A. Feta." *Sochineniia.* St. Peters-

burg: Panteon literatury, 1891, II, 352–94. First part of the
article is a general statement on esthetics by Botkin; the second
part is an essay on Fet, whom the critic terms "primarily a
nature poet." The article first appeared in 1857.

BUKHSHTAB, B. IA. "A. A. Fet," in Fet, *Polnoe sobranie stikhotvorenii.*
Leningrad: Sovetskii pisatel', 1959, pp. 5–78. An inclusive, in-
cisive, and intelligent treatment of the corpus of Fet's poetry.

————. "Sud'ba literaturnogo nasledstva A. A. Feta," *Literaturnoe
nasledstvo,* Moscow, 1935, vol. XXII–XXIV, 561–602. Provides
an overview of Fet's writings in poetry and prose as a pre-
paratory step to possible publication at some future point.

————. "Esteticheskie vzgliady Feta," *Literaturnaia ucheba,* No. 12
(1936), pp. 35–51. An excellent summary of Fet's views on
the nature of art based in large part upon his explicit writings
on esthetic subjects.

DARSKII, D. *'Radost' zemli.' Issledovanie liriki Feta.* Moscow: F.
Nekrasov, 1916. An impressionistic book-length study of Fet's
lyric poetry.

EIKHENBAUM, B. M. *Melodika russkogo liricheskogo stikha.* Petersburg: Obshchestvo izucheniia poeticheskogo iazyka, 1922, pp.
119–95. By far the longest chapter in this book by a leading
Russian formalist critic is given over to a detailed analysis of
the technical devices utilized by Fet in his verse. Reprinted in
Eikhenbaum, *O poezii.* Leningrad: Sovetskii pisatel', 1969.

GRIGOR'EV, A. A. "Russkaia iziashchnaia literatura v 1852 godu," in
Grigor'ev, *Literaturnaia kritika,* Moscow: Khudozhestvennaia
literatura, 1967, pp. 41–111. Includes a sensitive early appreciation of Fet's poetry by one of Russia's best critical minds.

GROMOV, P. P. "A. A. Fet," in Fet, *Stikhotvoreniia,* third edition,
Moscow-Leningrad: Sovetskii pisatel', 1963, pp. 5–88. A general
introduction to Fet's poetry and the critical response to his work.

————. *Blok, ego predshestvenniki i sovremenniki.* Leningrad:
Sovetskii pisatel', 1966, pp. 18–31. A detailed discussion of the
interrelationships between Fet's poetry and that of the young
Alexander Blok, who considered Fet his poetic mentor.

IAMPOL'SKII, I. G. "Poeziia shestidesiatykh godov (obshchii obzor),"
in *Istoriia russkoi literatury.* Moscow-Leningrad: Akademiia
nauk SSSR, 1956, vol. VIII, pt. 2, 7–55. An overview of Russian poetry of the 1860's by a senior specialist in the period
which helps to place Fet in the history of Russian poetry.

LOTMAN, L. M. "Liricheskaia i istoricheskaia poeziia 50–70–kh
godov," in *Istoriia russkoi poezii,* Leningrad: Nauka, 1969, II,

124–90. A general essay on the poetry of Fet, Apollon Maykov, Yakov Polonsky, Aleksey Tolstoy, Karolina Pavlova, and Lev Mey in the context of their times.

NEKRASOV, N. A. "Russkie vtorostepennye poety," in Nekrasov, *Polnoe sobranie sochinenii i pisem,* Moscow: Goslitizdat, 1950, vol. IX. A historic article by a great Russian poet in which Fet is mentioned, although the article is devoted mostly to Tyutchev.

NIKOL'SKII, B. V. "Osnovnye elementy liriki Feta," in Fet, *Polnoe sobranie stikhotvorenii.* St. Petersburg: A. F. Marks, 1912, I, 24–54. A detailed discussion of Fet's lyrics with special attention to their philosophical implications.

POLONSKII, IA. "Moi studencheskie vospominaniia." *Ezhemesiachnye literaturnye prilozheniia k Nive,* No. 12 (December 1898). Rather chatty memoirs of the 1840's by a poet who had known Fet, Grigorev and many others as young men.

SALTYKOV-SHCHEDRIN, M. E. "Stikhotvoreniia A. A. Feta," in Shchedrin, *Polnoe sobranie sochinenii,* Moscow-Leningrad: Gosudarstvennoe izdatel'stvo khudozhestvennoi literatury, 1937, V, 330–33. A sarcastic review of Fet's 1863 collection by a radical critic who rejects Fet's world as "rather narrow, monotonous, and limited."

————. "Nasha obshchestvennaia zhizn'," in Shchedrin, *Polnoe sobranie sochinenii,* Moscow-Leningrad, 1941, VI, 84–100. A satirical treatment of a political article by Fet, published in early 1863, in which Fet writes of economic conditions in the rural area where he lives.

SOLOV'EV, V. S. "O liricheskoi poezii. Po povodu poslednikh stikhotvorenii Feta i Polonskogo," in Solov'ev, *Sobranie sochinenii,* St. Petersburg: Obshchestvennaia pol'za, 1901, VI, 215–40. First published in 1890, the article attempts the ambitious task of defining the distinguishing characteristics of lyric poetry—as set apart from other types of poetry—on the basis of Fet's and Polonsky's most recent works.

STRAKHOV, N. N. "A. A. Fet. Biograficheskii ocherk," in Fet, *Polnoe sobranie stikhotvorenii.* St. Petersburg: A. F. Marks, 1912, I, 3–10. A quick survey of the chronology of Fet's life. Includes dates for the writing and publication of some of his works.

ZHIRMUNSKII, V. *Kompozitsiia liricheskikh stikhotvorenii.* Petrograd: Obshchestvo izucheniia poeticheskogo iazyka, 1921. A fundamental work in the formal analysis of poetic language, utilizing many examples taken from the poems of Fet as well as of other major Russian poets.

GUSTAFSON, R. F. *The Imagination of Spring: The Poetry of Afanasy Fet*. New Haven and London: Yale University Press, 1966. The only book on Fet in English and a principal contribution to scholarship on Fet. Close reading of Fet's poetry, elucidation of numerous literary influences and parallels.

Index

175